PAUL VALÉRY · CHARMS

By Peter Dale

EDGE TO EDGE
New and selected poems
ONE ANOTHER
UNDER THE BREATH

Translations

DANTE: THE DIVINE COMEDY
TRISTAN CORBIÈRE: WRY-BLUE LOVES
POEMS OF JULES LAFORGUE
POEMS OF FRANÇOIS VILLON

Prose

AN INTRODUCTION TO RHYME

Interviews

In conversation with Peter Dale

MICHAEL HAMBURGER
ANTHONY THWAITE
(with Ian Hamilton)
RICHARD WILBUR

In conversation with Cynthia Haven

PETER DALE

PAUL VALÉRY
Charms
and Other Pieces

Translated with introduction and notes by

Peter Dale

ANVIL PRESS POETRY

Published in 2007
by Anvil Press Poetry Ltd
Neptune House 70 Royal Hill London SE10 8RF
www.anvilpresspoetry.com

Translation, introduction and notes copyright © Peter Dale 2007

French text copyright © Editions Gallimard, Paris
Charmes © Gallimard 1922
Album de vers anciens © Gallimard 1920, 1927
La feuille blanche © Estate of Paul Valéry

This book is published with financial assistance
from Arts Council England

Designed and set in Monotype Ehrhardt by Anvil
Printed and bound in Great Britain
by Hobbs the Printers Ltd

ISBN 978 0 85646 398 3

A catalogue record for this book
is available from the British Library

ACKNOWLEDGEMENTS

Versions of parts of this translation have appeared in *Agenda*; *Modern European Poets*, Spiny Babbler, Nepal; *Orpheus*, Perros-Guirec, France, and *Quattrocento*, UK. The translator is grateful to the Hippopotamus Press for .permission to reprint versions revised from *Narrow Straits*. Parts of the introductory material were first published in *Orpheus*, Perros-Guirec, France, 2005.

The translator is extremely grateful to Jean-Pierre Attal for permission to make use of his researches into Valéry.

The text of Valéry's poems is reprinted by permission of Gallimard.

CONTENTS

Charms
Charmes

Other Pieces

A BRIEF LIFE OF VALÉRY

VALÉRY WAS BORN in 1871 in Sète on the Mediterranean coast of France. His father was Corsican, his mother Genoese. He was educated first by the Dominicans, then in the town school. His earliest verse was written in a school notebook while he dreamed of going to naval college. The family moved to Montpellier where he went to the *lycée* and on to the law faculty. Baudelaire's poems became one of his enthusiasms about this time. From around 1884 he was reading Huysmans, Verlaine and Rimbaud before being overwhelmed by the work of Mallarmé. At this stage he was also drawing and painting and had a keen interest in architecture and mathematics.

Around 1890 he made the acquaintance of Pierre Louÿs and André Gide, and published a few poems in symbolist magazines, chiefly 'Narcissus Speaks' from which 'Fragments of the "Narcissus"' derives. He spent time in Paris where Pierre Louÿs introduced him to Mallarmé.

However, during 4th and 5th October 1892, he experienced an emotional and intellectual crisis after which he gave up poetry.

In 1894 he moved to Paris and began attending Mallarmé's now famous Tuesdays in the rue de Rome. He was writing no verse but devoting the early hours of each day to deep thinking on a wide range of subjects recorded in notebooks which ran after twenty-nine years to 257 books. Little of this was published during his life-time.

In 1895 he published the later to be celebrated prose work, 'Introduction to the Method of Leonardo da Vinci', in *La Nouvelle Revue Française*, not collected until *Variété* in 1924.

He spent several months in England during 1894 and again in 1896. Here he met W. E. Henley and George Meredith and discussed Toulouse-Lautrec with Aubrey Beardsley. During this last period he wrote two articles which appeared in *The*

Art Journal, put into English by an anonymous translator. They were on the sculptor Paul Dubois and on some busts by Houdon discovered in Versailles. No French texts survive. (A notebook of Valéry's concerning the first visit, *1984: Carnet Inédit – Dit 'Carnet de Londres'*, edited by Florence de Lussy, was published by Gallimard in 2005.)

Between 1897 and 1899 he worked as an editor for the Ministry of War. He spent much spare time among the impressionist painters. The death of Mallarmé in 1898 affected him deeply.

In 1900 he married Jeannie Gobillard, a niece of the painter Berthe Morisot. They had two sons, Claude and François, and a daughter, Agathe. Through the good offices of a friend, André Lebey, he was made personal secretary to Édouard Lebey, administrator of the Havas agency, a post which allowed him a large amount of time free to pursue his own work. He remained in the post until 1922 when Lebey died.

In 1912 André Gide and the publisher Gallimard pestered him to collect his early verse. He contemplated writing a 'Farewell to Poetry'. However he became deeply involved with verse again and wrote the complex poem, 'La Jeune Parque'.

To distract himself from the war, he set about revising, polishing and ordering his early poems; he also began writing others. 'La Jeune Parque' ('The Young Fate') appeared in 1917 and, in 1920, *Album of Early Verses* followed. After *Charms* had appeared to great acclaim in 1922, curiously the same year as *The Waste Land*, he more or less gave poetry up for prose again, concentrating on mathematics, aesthetics, artists, writers and the nature of the self – another major theme of the verse.

In 1923 he published two dialogues: *Eupalinos or the Architect* and *The Soul and the Dance*. A collection of essays, *Variety*, appeared in 1924, a title that was retained for further collections: vol. II, 1929; vol. III in 1936; vol. IV in 1938, and vol. V in 1944.

In 1925 he was elected to the French Academy. In 1933 he became administrator of the University Mediterranean Centre in Nice.

The prose work of 1896 'La Soirée avec Monsieur Teste' ('The Evening with Monsieur Teste') was collected with other essays to appear in *Monsieur Teste* in 1926.

In 1931 his melodrama *Amphion* was performed at the Opéra, followed in 1934 by another, *Semiramis,* both to music by Honegger.

During the Second World War, he published various extracts from his prose journals, two with a name that caught on, *Tel quel I* and *Tel quel II*. In 1942 he spoke a eulogy at the Academy for the philosopher Henri Bergson, disregarding the climate of Nazi anti-Semitism. The Vichy government reacted by removing him from his post.

On 26th August 1944 he watched the celebration march of the Liberation of Paris. In this year he completed what was to be his last poetic endeavour, a prose poem, 'He became the Angel', written up from a draft of 1922. He died in Paris on 20th July 1945 and was buried with national mourning in the cemetery at Sète, location of 'Le cimetière marin' ('The Graveyard by the Sea').

INTRODUCTION

DESPITE THE FACT that he opposed the idea that poems could be put in any other form of words but their own, Valéry is one of the most studied of French poets, not least by himself.

He said of *Charms*, in his introduction to an annotated version of it by Alain, that his verse had the sense that anyone gives to it and that the sense he gave to it was to suit him only and displaced no one else's. He did not see why poems should have either a fixed sense or a final text. He insisted that it was a mistake against the nature of poetry, possibly even the death of it, to pretend that any poem had a meaning that corresponded to something verifiable and unique matching some thought of the author's.

Such remarks, seemingly a gift to exegetes and translators, are not an endorsement of a type of post-modernist indeterminacy. Nor are they as go-as-you-please as they look. What Valéry always insisted on was that the stuff of poems was not mere words and definitions which could be rearranged into other words. His idea of the poem derives ultimately from the overwhelming impression the poems of Mallarmé made on him in his youth. He wrote, after having received copies of some of Mallarmé's poems, that, leaving for the coast with them in his hands, the full sun, the dazzling road, the blue sky, and scents of plants scorching were as nothing to him then, so absorbed was he by verses he considered unprecedented. He was always a lover of sea and sun, but their hold was nothing then in the presence of these poems which he felt in his deepest self.

He considered that Mallarmé possessed the most powerful quality for original poetry: the magic formula, the ability to make words incantatory. (One of the reasons for Valéry's title *Charms*.) The poem was to be like a spell or piece of music, a unitary experience contained only in itself and to be received whole. He remarked that the efficacy of 'charms' lay not in the signification deriving from their terms but in their resonances and the individualities of their form. He considered that a degree of obscurity itself was almost essential to them. In summary, he thought poems were for making us 'become' not for making us 'understand'. The process first of making the poem, then of the reader's taking it in, was in many senses for him the poem itself. Broadly speaking that remained Valéry's approach.

Consequently he considered any idea that poetry should be engaged in efforts for social or political change or be otherwise put to some practical use was mistaken. The poet's duty was to the poem. He also insisted that verse is not an outpouring of feeling, not a question of the personal emotions or the living personality of the writer.

Yet, in what some may feel an unexpected contrast to his musical-incantatory view, he is classical in his approach to form and matter in verse. A brilliant metricist in the traditional syllabic traditions of France, he is also content to use at times archaistic forms and diction, employing sometimes the more Latinate senses of French words. On the other hand he is humorous, witty, sly and oblique in his work, aspects which sometimes suggest the Metaphysicals. He appears to insist that poetry is a matter of form and style and, in terms of inspiration, at most the patient development of a *donné*. Some of these will be mentioned in the notes for particular poems.

However, there is almost a sort of schizophrenia in his work between the mystery of poetic inspiration, obsession, and the demand for total control of the outcome. He could not always keep these forces in useful equilibrium within a single poem. In summary he said in his essay 'Concerning Corot' that spontaneity in art is the spoils of conquest.

This two-way pull in his work has drawn mixed response even in France. In his essay 'Lines of Force in French Poetry' Paul Emmanuel first cites Claudel who wrote: 'Paul Valéry was intent throughout his life on denying inspiration.' Emmanuel, who had studied the tortuous development in manuscript of

Valéry's 'La Jeune Parque', 'The Young Fate', then continues: 'I do not know of anyone who, as much as Valéry, laboured so externally at what he produced. One may be permitted to think that rarely has labour been so much in vain.'

Yet Valéry's basic poetic ideas were simple. He believed that from a *donné*, some rhythm or other accident of language or thought, a poem might take off, whereupon the task of the poet was to use his full intellect to shape and direct the ideas that poetry might draw from the dark depths of the soul and the mystery of life. Yet he did not trust simply the muse, a lax attitude he found in most other poets. He believed intense scrutiny of the deepest self could dredge up creative material in developing the *donné*. Thereafter he believed in the importance of form in quarrying and making sense of the inchoate matter drawn up. He often uses the dark earth to symbolise the unconscious and the bright sun to symbolise the shaping consciousness. A favourite image of intelligence and poetry was the tree with its depths in the earth but its foliage seeking the sun, forever thwarted in the attempt to penetrate the sky to reach a state where the division between self and exterior reality was closed in unity of being.

Given those ideas, he nevertheless remained an atheist. Ultimately he believed poems necessarily failed to achieve this perfection of form; that intellect never could fully master the process; that the self developed in making the poem and that the self now different would want to reach further development through and beyond that particular text. He remarked, in 'Degas Dance Drawing', that prolonged contemplation of any of the arts deepens into insoluble problems; that long scrutiny gives rise to an infinite amount of difficulties, imaginary impasses, opposed wishes, doubts and scruples in ratio with the intelligence and experience of the artist. Hence, presumably, his long silences. In the end he became absorbed in the process of digging into the self for the work, observing the self in process of composing and in all the vagaries of the development of the poem. Critics have deplored this attitude but critical books of the period, such as J. L. Lowes' *The Road to Xanadu*, 1927, on the genesis of 'The Ancient Mariner', seem equally to relish the weird processing that goes on in the poet's creative thinking – some might even think to the detriment of the actual poems under investigation. Valéry had the same fascination. He actually remarked that all criticism has been dominated by the threadbare principle that the artist is the cause of the work as a criminal is considered the cause of his crime. Both he considered to be the effects of what they do.

These proclivities in some ways make him a puzzling poet. The musical-incantatory view of poetry has most often been propounded by poets who, not to put too fine a point on it, might be considered somewhat weaker in the brain-pan than their colleagues: Swinburne, Verlaine, Dylan Thomas, Tennyson perhaps. But Valéry considered himself to have a powerful intellect. He enjoyed from his extensive years of writing prose the reputation of a deep and original thinker. The poems, then, are not Swinburnian effusions of fairly general emotion. They use ideas that are deeply and vividly felt and often present them very concretely. The poems relish their brilliances of stylistic mastery over his narrow range of ideas, a range obsessively limited when compared with that of the prose works. His treatment in verse of some of these ideas in one or two of the short poems may sometimes seem too elaborated, fanciful or Gallic to some English-speaking readers. Yet for all the insistence on intelligent composition he seems to have been fairly obsessive in his concerns.

It is never wise to take a poet's obiter dicta without the odd pinch of salt. Valéry is also the poet of the Mediterranean French coast. He has said, in 'Mediterranean Inspirations', that nothing had formed him more, indwelt him more deeply, better instructed him than the hours stolen from study, apparently wandering but devoted fundamentally to the unconscious cult of three or four incontestable deities. These were the sea, sky and sun. His poems celebrate and emblemize sun, sea, women, food, wine, scintillating light, trees of all sorts. Finally they celebrate the life, the liveliness within themselves, their escape from silence. The more playful Auden and Wallace Stevens sometimes seem good parallels. Compared to the somewhat cold crystal quality of Mallarmé he is the poet of scintillating sea, dazzling sun and bright colour, all deeply felt.

Valéry is in the main stream of French sensibilities, a subtle range of scents which are difficult to net in English words – like the bouquet of a good wine. The poems *delight* in mind, in themselves, in a light and intellectual wit, in a rather rhetorical style and form uncommon in the poetic traditions of English. Also, unlike so much English language poetry, they are not chary of abstractions. They impishly draw attention to their own movement in terms of sound effects and 'felicities'. They have a sly wit that seems sometimes to be sending the poems up when not sending up possible readers, scholars and exegetes.

English lyric is often a thing to be eavesdropped. Valéry's poems may be soliloquies but they are spoken straight at the audience by consummate actors, revelling in their skills.

The poet closest to the position of Valéry in the English-speaking world as just suggested is probably Wallace Stevens. Eliot admired the poet but was very different in his approach. In his introduction to the second volume of Valéry's translated collected works, *The Art of Poetry*, he remarked that Valéry's theory of poetics 'provides us with no criterion of seriousness'. He may be right but it is not a criticism of what Valéry was directly trying to do. Valéry's was a different seriousness from his. Valéry thought the process of writing and reading a poem, as indicated above, was in itself the experience and commented on nothing external to it.

In his essay, 'Eugenio Montale', Leavis had suggested that, in fact, Eliot's own development had been towards Valéry, and cited a 1924 introduction of Eliot's to Valéry's poem, later to be called 'Sketch of a Serpent': 'To reduce one's disorderly and mostly silly personality to the gravity of a *jeu de quilles* [game of skittles], would be to do an excellent thing.' This seems a quick version of Eliot's doctrine of the impersonality of art.

Leavis in his essay also remarked with the usual British impatience: 'Poetry that conceives itself as a *jeu de quilles*, however strenuous, cannot be lived with; before long it becomes boring – as, I confess, for all the brilliance I have so admired, I find "Le Cimetière marin" and "Ebauche d'un serpent".' However, in 'Questions de Poésie' (*Variété* III), Valéry comments on those arbiters with no appetite for poetry who end up judging and explaining it – 'the consequences of which are fearful'.

The influence of Valéry on Eliot was also noted by Donald Davie: 'From "Prufrock" to "Little Gidding" is a movement from Laforgue to Valéry.' It was part of: '... the late-Romantic ambition, which according to Valéry over-rode all else in French *symbolisme*, the will to make poetry approach the condition of music... as the title, *Four Quartets*, triumphantly declares.'

Wallace Stevens, a great Francophile, could not have missed the literary vibrations of Valéry, it might be thought. However, in his letters, for a considerable time he took pains to play down any direct influence. In a letter to the mysterious Ronald Lane Latimer, 5 November 1935, he wrote: '... Valéry's *Etat de la vertu*, beautifully printed by Léon Pichon... I have had it in my room under my eye... but I have not read a line of it. If there is any relation in my things to Valéry's, it must come about in some such way as this...' – This is light-hearted but somewhat ambivalent for, without further reference to Valéry, he then discusses the difficulty of getting away from abstract thought into poetry proper in relation to his 'statue' poems where the symbol changes significance from poem to poem. The implication seems to be that such influence as Valéry may have exerted was more or less in the air of the period to be absorbed by anyone sensitive enough to it. He was saying much the same thing in correspondence in the mid forties. But in later letters from about 1952 when he begins to read Valéry's own correspondence the references become more open and admiring and it is clear he had begun more serious reading of Valéry. He had a fine copy of Alain's annotated *Charmes* and became interested enough to accept an invitation to introduce two of the Socratic prose dialogues for the collected American edition of Valéry's complete works. His introduction to 'Eupalinos' gives in a brief space a fine summary of most of Valéry's major ideas and obsessions, the architectural idea controlling much of the poet's approach.

Stevens, in his concluding remarks, quotes in translation from 'Eupalinos' the following passage: 'What is there more mysterious than clarity? ... What more capricious than the way in which light and shade are distributed over hours and over men? ... Orpheuslike we build, by means of the word, temples of wisdom and science that may suffice all reasonable creatures. This great art requires of us an admirably exact language.' The passage may well be applied to Valéry's approach to poetic creation, not just to architecture. (His poems fairly often make use of architectural imagery.)

Valéry's most enthusiastic English-speaking critic was probably Yvor Winters. In 'Problems for the Modern Critic of Literature', he actually asserted: '... *Le Cimetière Marin* and *Ébauche d'un Serpent* ... so far as my knowledge and judgement will guide me, are the two greatest short poems ever written. The first of these is the simpler to grasp, and hence better known. The second is the greater.' Yet on the way to this judgement he was fairly unimpressed by the even shorter poems and by Valéry's reputation as an original thinker.

The poet Michael Hamburger in his *The Truth of Poetry* cites a remark by Valéry in 'As I was saying to Mallarmé' (*Variété* III, Gallimard, 1936). Valéry wrote that Mallarmé's syntax makes the structure of expressions more felt and more interesting than their significance or value. Hamburger also quotes a rather testy response to the idea by Donald Davie: 'The syntax of Mallarmé appeals to nothing but itself, to nothing outside the world of the poem.' – It is more or less an opposing version of

Eliot's admiring criticism of Valéry quoted above. Valéry's response might well have been his own impatient: *Ce que l'on peut conter ne compte que fort peu* (Things that may be recounted don't count for very much). Davie has more to say on this issue of syntax, particularly Valéry's, in his book *Articulate Energy*.

Nevertheless a degree of impatience with Valéry's verse is a feeling that a reader may experience in perusing some of the minor poems. The long poems may pack a punch more considerable than their reach but some of the shorter pieces seem to be, despite their musicality, over-elaborate for what they appear to be. 'The Rower' for example seems more concerned with its movement through syntax and sound than in the rather thin idea extended in such a leisurely fashion. No amount of symbolic interpretation seems able to dispel this feeling. The symbol is so indulged that it begins to lose the actuality where it began without gaining much for the loss. If the poem were ever going to work it should have been more succinct.

Perhaps in no poet of status was there such a gap between the masterpieces and the make-weights. Valéry's major reputation will rest, as Winters detected, on 'The Graveyard by the Sea', and 'Sketch of a Serpent'. Another large work, 'The Pythoness', is also a powerful dramatic monologue the conclusion of which is weakened by what feels more like the poet speaking, though Valéry did admit that the pythoness was not likely to speak ideas in a continuous and extended syntax as is represented in the poem. The monologue does for the most part maintain the reader's suspension of disbelief. Some of the visual and sound effects are extremely powerful.

Of the first of these three poems, Valéry claimed that it was more or less taken out of his hands one morning when he was at work on it by the editor Jacques Rivière who wished to publish it as it stood. The poet surrendered the piece with the feeling that a work was never perfected but merely abandoned. There are uneven passages he may well have worked on if he had been left to it. He had spent years on it up until then.

A meditation on the graveyard at Sète on the Mediterranean coast where he was born, 'The Graveyard by the Sea' is an elegy in the Thomas Gray tradition on the generality of death. It weaves in and out of Valéry's habitual imagery: his silence; the self and its relation to externals: the sun, the sea, consciousness versus the inanimate; traditional memorials and the tragedy of extinction. It closes with a turning back to life as the wind invigorates the sea. The poem scintillates with light and the movement of sun and shadow, noises of the sea; it has touches of humour and some arid passages that seem too abstractly worked over. The most powerful passage is somewhat reminiscent of Villon's *Testament* – verses 176–178, in the Anvil edition numbering of the text and translation. C. Day Lewis, a translator of the elegy, commenting on the same passage, wrote that Valéry might well 'be accounted, in the final reckoning, a superb artist rather than a great poet. Yet the six tremendous stanzas of *Le Cimetière marin*, beginning "Les morts cachés sont bien dans cette terre", speak profoundly out of the human condition.' Paradoxically, the passage referred to is in several ways the least Valéryan of his work.

'Sketch of a Serpent' is probably his most finished poem, if we allow a term the poet himself doubted. It presents the dramatic monologue of the Garden of Eden serpent shown as a rather know-all wide boy out to spoil God's little game. The poem uses disjunctive registers of language with deliberate disparities and bathos, along with an equally deliberate elaboration of sound-effects. The theme is the Gnostic one that the creation was a diminution of God's essence and that the development of consciousness trapped in it was the big flaw. While all this is going on, it also celebrates the animal pleasures of existence in presenting sun and the sensual enjoyment of colour and movement. The serpent's sensuous description of the naked Eve and her movement is all that there is to indicate Adam.

This serpent is 'He who modifies'. It is tempting to see at least a little of Valéry in his serpent's self-description when he makes remarks to the effect that he considered work [in composition] itself as having a value of its own superior to that which people in general attach to the product or result. On the other hand, Auden, in his essay 'The Joker in the Pack', remarked that the quotation was 'the ideal motto, surely, for Iago's coat of arms.'

In his essay 'On the Nude' Valéry wrote of the Fall: 'We will not look into the metaphysical consequences of that fatal moment ... but many other effects arose from the same cause.' He adds that nothing is more remarkable, more worthy of contemplation than the strange fecundity of an act of free will and he concludes that all our law, customs and arts derive from the Fall.

The 'Fragments of the "Narcissus"' is probably the least impressive of the great poems in its appeal to Anglo-Saxon sensibility. It elaborates well beyond the scope of its material the myth of the self-love of Narcissus. Valéry remarked at a conference in 1941, however, that the theme of Narcissus that he had chosen was a sort of poetic autobiography. It is true that he was absorbed at times in a solipsist view of the world, rather like Wordsworth who had to grab a gate-post as a child to make sure that external substance existed. The poem is a leisurely proceeding and the myth seems more a peg on which to hang some admittedly fine writing, using the classical French alexandrine, than a compelling poem. One can understand both its attraction for Valéry and his abandonment of the attempt to finish the piece.

There remains, however, some truth in Allen Tate's remark, in 'A Note on Paul Valéry', that he was a greater poet than his intellect wanted him to be.

In his essay 'Mr Housman at Little Bethel' in his *Literary Essays*, Ezra Pound remarked: 'Saxpence reward for any authenticated case of intellect having stopped a chap writing poesy! You might as well claim that railway tracks stop the engine. No one ever claimed they would make it go.' Valéry's high regard for his own intelligence seems sometimes to have marshalled him into sidings where he could not deliver all the poems his talent seemed capable of unloading.

Yet it may have been neither Valéry's intellect nor his pursuit of an impossible perfection that kept his poetic oeuvre so small. As recorded by George Seferis in his preface to Igor Stravinsky's *Poetics of Music*, T. S. Eliot concluded a conversation they had about Valéry by saying: 'He was so intelligent that he had no ambition at all.'

PETER DALE

A NOTE ON THE TEXT AND TRANSLATION

Attempts have been made by some scholars to find an overall structure to *Charms* but in the first edition the poems were published in more or less alphabetical order. Subsequent editions were rearranged and the order finally retained was as here. The last two parts of 'Fragments of the "Narcissus"' were not added until the edition of 1926. The order of stanzas in 'The Graveyard by the Sea' had been altered in various editions.

Valéry is an extremely formal, musical poet so that it seemed inescapable that he should be translated into English forms which would mirror the formal qualities of his French as far as is possible across the rather different traditional prosodies of the two languages. Where these differences create a major variation in formal approaches this has been indicated in notes to the poems in question. For similar reasons and with similar problems rhyme has been retained.

I am grateful to Kit Yee Wong for checking the French text.

P.D.

A BRIEF READING LIST

The Collected Works of Paul Valéry, in translation, edited by Jackson Mathews, Bollingen Series XLV, 1960.

Variété III, Gallimard, 1936 is almost essential background material to *Charms* and for Valéry's ideas on Mallarmé, poetry in general, and his Mediterranean origins. It is also available in translation in the collection mentioned above.

Selected Writings of Paul Valéry, no editor named, New Directions, New York, 1964. This contains translations of poems by various hands, including some in free verse and prose not given in this translation, and extracts of the prose. The selection is based on *Morceaux choisis*, made by Valéry himself.

The Function of Criticism, Yvor Winters, Alan Swallow, Denver, 1957, the first essay.

Memories and Essays Old and New 1926–1974, Allen Tate, Carcanet, Manchester, 1976: 'A Note on Paul Valéry'.

Articulate Energy, Donald Davie, Routledge & Kegan Paul, 1976.

The Truth of Poetry, Michael Hamburger, Anvil, 1996.

The Poet's Work, ed. Reginald Gibbons, Houghton Mifflin, Boston, 1979: 'A Poet's Notebook', Paul Valéry, translated by Denise Folliot.

French Poetry 1820–1950 edited and translated by William Rees, Penguin Classics, 1990: basic prose versions of eight of Valéry's poems, including 'The Graveyard by the Sea'.

The Penguin Book of French Verse, 1975, by various editors, containing basic prose versions by Anthony Hartley of 'Narcissus Speaks', 'To the Plane Tree', 'The Sylphe' and 'The Graveyard by the Sea'.

Charms

Charmes

AURORE

à Paul Poujaud.

La confusion morose
Qui me servait de sommeil,
Se dissipe dès la rose
Apparence du soleil.
Dans mon âme je m'avance,
Tout ailé de confiance:
C'est la première oraison!
A peine sorti des sables,
Je fais des pas admirables
Dans les pas de ma raison.

Salut! encore endormies
A vos sourires jumeaux,
Similitudes amies
Qui brillez parmi les mots!
Au vacarme des abeilles
Je vous aurai par corbeilles,
Et sur l'échelon tremblant
De mon échelle dorée,
Ma prudence évaporée
Déjà pose son pied blanc.

Quelle aurore sur ces croupes
Qui commencent de frémir!
Déjà s'étirent par groupes
Telles qui semblaient dormir:
L'une brille, l'autre bâille;
Et sur un peigne d'écaille,
Égarant ses vagues doigts,
Du songe encore prochaine,

DAWN

to Paul Poujaud

The glum confusing doze
That serves as sleep for me
Dissipates with the rose-
Pink sun's ascendency.
My spirit gathers sense
On wings of confidence:
The first prayer of the day!
Hardly out of the sand,
Wonderful steps I land
And tread on reason's way.

Welcome, still dozy broods,
To your twin smiles, you herds
Of friendly similitudes
That sparkle among words!
And to you buzzing bees,
In hives, I say, not trees;
On my golden ladder put –
Away all caution flung –
On to the trembling rung
Already a bare foot.

What daybreak on these rumps
That start to wiggle, shake!
At once they stretch their stumps
Though only just awake:
One shines; one gives a yawn;
One's stray fingers drawn
To a comb of tortoise-shell;
Dreamy, the idler toys,

La paresseuse l'enchaîne
Aux prémisses de sa voix.

Quoi! c'est vous, mal déridées!
Que fîtes-vous, cette nuit,
Maîtresses de l'âme, Idées,
Courtisanes par ennui?
– Toujours sages, disent-elles,
Nos présences immortelles
Jamais n'ont trahi ton toit!
Nous étions non éloignées,
Mais secrètes araignées
Dans les ténèbres de toi!

Ne seras-tu pas de joie
Ivre! à voir de l'ombre issus
Cent mille soleils de soie
Sur tes énigmes tissus?
Regarde ce que nous fîmes:
Nous avons sur tes abîmes
Tendu nos fils primitifs,
Et pris la nature nue
Dans une trame ténue
De tremblants préparatifs...

Leur toile spirituelle,
Je la brise, et vais cherchant
Dans ma forêt sensuelle
Les oracles de mon chant.
Être! Universelle oreille!
Toute l'âme s'appareille
A l'extrême du désir...
Elle s'écoute qui tremble
Et parfois ma lèvre semble
Son frémissement saisir.

The premises of her voice
Bewitch it in their spell.

What! It's you, rumpled frizz!
What did you do last night,
Ideas, soul-mistresses,
Whoring in boredom's spite?
– We're always good in essence
And our immortal presence
Did nothing to betray
Your house! We've been insiders,
Not far off, secret spiders,
In your self shadows lay!

Drunk! won't you be with delight!
To see from shadows issue
A hundred thousand bright
Silk suns on your puzzle tissue?
Look what we have done:
Over your chasms spun
Our primitive tiny braids,
And taken nature plain
Into a tenuous skein
Of trembling ready-mades...

Their spiritual web I breach
And go through, searching long
My sensuous forest to reach
The oracles of my song.
Being! Universal Hearing!
The whole soul set to nearing
Desire's utmost aim...
Trembling, herself she hears.
Sometimes my lip appears
That thrill of hers to claim.

Voici mes vignes ombreuses,
Les berceaux de mes hasards!
Les images sont nombreuses
A l'égal de mes regards…
Toute feuille me présente
Une source complaisante
Où je bois ce frêle bruit…
Tout m'est pulpe, tout amande.
Tout calice me demande
Que j'attende pour son fruit.

Je ne crains pas les épines!
L'éveil est bon, même dur!
Ces idéales rapines
Ne veulent pas qu'on soit sûr:
Il n'est pour ravir un monde
De blessure si profonde
Qui ne soit au ravisseur
Une féconde blessure,
Et son propre sang l'assure
D'être le vrai possesseur.

J'approche la transparence
De l'invisible bassin
Où nage mon Espérance
Que l'eau porte par le sein.
Son col coupe le temps vague
Et soulève cette vague
Que fait un col sans pareil…
Elle sent sous l'onde unie
La profondeur infinie,
Et frémit depuis l'orteil.

Here are my shady vines,
Cradling my lucky chances!
The images and signs
As countless as my glances ...
Every leaf offers me
A source willing and free
To sip at sounds minute ...
All pulp, all kernel, grist.
All chalices insist
I wait until they fruit.

No fear of barbs I feel!
Waking's good, a hard cure!
These raids of the ideal
Don't want you being sure:
It is to ravish a realm,
So deeply overwhelm,
That on the ravisher light
A blow so fruitful his own
Blood proves that he alone
Possesses it by right.

The transparence I near
Of the invisible pool
In which my Hope swims clear
In the water's bosom cool.
Her throat breaks the vague time,
Makes with a throat sublime
That wake ... The waters close;
She feels the boundless deeps
Beneath her and there creeps
A tremble up from her toes.

AU PLATANE

à *André Fontainas.*

Tu penches, grand Platane, et te proposes nu,
      Blanc comme un jeune Scythe,
Mais ta candeur est prise, et ton pied retenu
      Par la force du site.

Ombre retentissante en qui le même azur
      Qui t'emporte, s'apaise,
La noire mère astreint ce pied natal et pur
      A qui la fange pèse.

De ton front voyageur les vents ne veulent pas;
      La terre tendre et sombre,
O Platane, jamais ne laissera d'un pas
      S'émerveiller ton ombre!

Ce front n'aura d'accès qu'aux degrés lumineux
      Où la sève l'exalte;
Tu peux grandir, candeur, mais non rompre les nœuds
      De l'éternelle halte!

Pressens autour de toi d'autres vivants liés
      Par l'hydre vénérable;
Tes pareils sont nombreux, des pins aux peupliers,
      De l'yeuse à l'érable,

Qui, par les morts saisis, les pieds échevelés
      Dans la confuse cendre,
Sentent les fuir les fleurs, et leurs spermes ailés
      Le cours léger descendre.

THE PLANE TREE

to André Fontainas

You lean, great Plane Tree; naked, yourself propose
    Like a young Scythian, white,
And yet your candour's caught, your held foot undergoes
    The strong restraint of the site.

Resonant shadow, in which the very azure that
    Carries you off's appeased,
The dark mother constrains that pure and newborn foot
    The weight of mire has seized.

The winds want nothing of your journeying brow.
    The earth, dark, tender base,
O Plane Tree, will never to your shade allow
    The marvel of a pace!

That brow will only reach the height of shining spots
    To which the sap may exalt;
You may grow taller, candour, yet not break the knots
    Of that eternal halt!

Sense around you other living beings bound
    By the revered hydra; pine
To poplar, holly-oak to maple; all around,
    Your peers you may divine,

Who, seized on by the dead, with feet dishevelled in
    The ashes mingled there,
All feel their blossom fly away, their winged seed spin
    Down light currents of air.

Le tremble pur, le charme, et ce hêtre formé
De quatre jeunes femmes,
Ne cessent point de battre un ciel toujours fermé,
Vêtus en vain de rames.

Ils vivent séparés, il pleurent confondus
Dans une seule absence,
Et leurs membres d'argent sont vainement fendus
A leur douce naissance.

Quand l'âme lentement qu'ils expirent le soir
Vers l'Aphrodite monte,
La vierge doit dans l'ombre, en silence, s'asseoir,
Toute chaude de honte.

Elle se sent surprendre, et pâle, appartenir
A ce tendre présage
Qu'une présente chair tourne vers l'avenir
Par un jeune visage...

Mais toi, de bras plus purs que les bras animaux,
Toi qui dans l'or les plonges,
Toi qui formes au jour le fantôme des maux
Que le sommeil fait songes,

Haute profusion de feuilles, trouble fier
Quand l'âpre tramontane
Sonne, au comble de l'or, l'azur du jeune hiver
Sur tes harpes, Platane,

Ose gémir!... Il faut, ô souple chair du bois,
Te tordre, te détordre,
Te plaindre sans te rompre, et rendre aux vents la voix
Qu'ils cherchent en désordre!

The pure aspen, the hornbeam, and this beech composed
　　Of four young women's stances,
Never cease to beat against a sky forever closed,
　　Arrayed in vain with branches.

They live in separation, mingled they lament
　　In one absence reft,
And at their gentle birth their silver limbs were rent
　　Apart and vainly cleft.

When slowly in the evening the soul they breathe
　　To Aphrodite rises,
The virgin, flushed all hot with shame, must sit beneath
　　The shade in mute surmises.

She feels herself surprised, and, pale, belonging to
　　That omen of tenderness
That present flesh is turning to the future through
　　A young complexion's guess...

Yet you, with arms more pure than animate arms,
　　Who plunge them through the gold,
You who form by day the ghosts of evils, harms
　　Turned dream when sleep takes hold,

Lofty profusion of leaves, haughty discomposure
　　When the harsh tramontane plies,
At the high point of the gold, upon your harps, the azure
　　Of the young winter's skies,

Tree, dare to groan!... You must, you supple ligneous flesh,
　　Twist and untwist in torture,
Complain and without breaking give the winds' thresh
　　The voice they seek in disorder!

Flagelle-toi!… Parais l'impatient martyr
                Qui soi-même s'écorche,
Et dispute à la flamme impuissante à partir
                Ses retours vers la torche!

Afin que l'hymne monte aux oiseaux qui naîtront,
                Et que le pur de l'âme
Fasse frémir d'espoir les feuillages d'un tronc
                Qui rêve de la flamme,

Je t'ai choisi, puissant personnage d'un parc,
                Ivre de ton tangage,
Puisque le ciel t'exerce, et te presse, ô grand arc,
                De lui rendre un langage!

O qu'amoureusement des Dryades rival,
                Le seul poète puisse
Flatter ton corps poli comme il fait du Cheval
                L'ambitieuse cuisse!…

– Non, dit l'arbre. Il dit: *Non!* par l'étincellement
                De sa tête superbe,
Que la tempête traite universellement
                Comme elle fait une herbe!

Self-flagellate!... As the impatient martyr show,
    Who scourges in self-torture,
Dispute against the flame powerless to go,
    Its reverting into torch!

So that, to birds near birth, the hymn may rise and aim,
    And so the pure in soul
May make the foliage of a trunk that dreams of flame
    Shudder in hope of goal,

Powerful parkland dweller, I have chosen you,
    Drunk with your turbulence,
Great bow, because the sky exerts you to endue
    It with a language, sense!

O, to the Dryads lovingly a rival force,
    May only the poet caress
And stroke your polished body as he does with the Horse
    The flanks' ambitiousness!...

– No, says the tree. It says: *No!* by the sparkling say
    Of its magnificent head
The tempest universally treats in the same way
    As grass beneath its tread!

CANTIQUE DES COLONNES

à Léon-Paul Fargue.

Douces colonnes, aux
Chapeaux garnis de jour
Ornés de vrais oiseaux
Qui marchent sur le tour,

Douces colonnes, ô
L'orchestre de fuseaux!
Chacun immole son
Silence à l'unisson.

– Que portez-vous si haut,
Égales radieuses?
– Au désir sans défaut
Nos grâces studieuses!

Nous chantons à la fois
Que nous portons les cieux!
O seule et sage voix
Qui chantes pour les yeux!

Vois quels hymnes candides!
Quelle sonorité
Nos éléments limpides
Tirent de la clarté!

Si froides et dorées
Nous fûmes de nos lits
Par le ciseau tirées,
Pour devenir ces lys!

CANTICLE OF THE COLUMNS

to Léon-Paul Fargue

O sweet columns, in
Hats bedecked with light,
Festooned with genuine
Birds that stroll your height,

O sweet columns, a
Stave orchestra!
The silence of each one
Blended in unison.

– So, what is it you wear,
You bright peers so exalted?
– Our studied graces air
In desire unfaulted!

We sing in unison
That we wear the skies!
O voice wise and one,
That's singing for the eyes!

What candid hymns we make!
What sonority, see,
Our clear elements take
Out of lucidity!

So gilded and so chill,
We were, out of our rest
Taken with chiselled skill
To be these lilies dressed!

De nos lits de cristal
Nous fûmes éveillées
Des griffes de métal
Nous ont appareillées.

Pour affronter la lune,
La lune et le soleil,
On nous polit chacune
Comme ongle de l'orteil!

Servantes sans genoux,
Sourires sans figures,
La belle devant nous
Se sent les jambes pures,

Pieusement pareilles,
Le nez sous le bandeau
Et nos riches oreilles
Sourdes au blanc fardeau,

Un temple sur les yeux
Noirs pour l'éternité,
Nous allons sans les dieux
A la divinité!

Nos antiques jeunesses,
Chair mate et belles ombres,
Sont fières des finesses
Qui naissent par les nombres!

Filles des nombres d'or,
Fortes des lois du ciel,
Sur nous tombe et s'endort
Un dieu couleur de miel.

From beds of crystal slabs
We have been roused from night.
The clutch of metal grabs
Caught us and trimmed us right.

To match us with the moon,
The moon, and with the sun,
We're polished to attune,
Like toe-nails, every one!

Maids without the knees,
Smiles without the face,
The beauty with us shes
Is purest leg in grace,

Religiously as peers,
Our noses fillet-topped,
And our expensive ears
Deaf with white weight stopped,

A temple on the eyes
Black for eternity,
Godlessly we rise
Towards divinity!

Antiquated she-youths,
Flesh dull and shadows fine,
We are proud of truths
By numbers born in line!

Daughters of golden miens,
With heaven's law strong-thewed,
On us there lights and leans
A god that's honey-hued.

Il dort content, le Jour,
Que chaque jour offrons
Sur la table d'amour
Étale sur nos fronts.

Incorruptibles sœurs,
Mi-brûlantes, mi-fraîches,
Nous prîmes pour danseurs
Brises et feuilles sèches,

Et les siècles par dix,
Et les peuples passés,
C'est un profond jadis,
Jadis jamais assez!

Sous nos mêmes amours
Plus lourdes que le monde
Nous traversons les jours
Comme une pierre l'onde!

Nous marchons dans le temps
Et nos corps éclatants
Ont des pas ineffables
Qui marquent dans les fables...

He sleeps content above,
The Light each day we offer
Upon the table of love
Set upon our coiffeur.

Incorruptible sisters,
Half ardent, half a freeze,
For dancers we had misters
Of the dead leaves and breeze,

And centuries in tens,
And peoples come and gone,
It is a deep long hence,
And hence for ever on!

Under our own loves more
Heavy than the world's weight,
We cross the days from yore,
As stone, the waves! Straight,

We're marching right through time.
The awesome stride sublime
Of our bedazzling physique
Appears in myths antique...

L'ABEILLE

à Francis de Miomandre.

Quelle, et si fine, et si mortelle,
Que soit ta pointe, blonde abeille,
Je n'ai, sur ma tendre corbeille,
Jeté qu'un songe de dentelle.

Pique du sein la gourde belle,
Sur qui l'Amour meurt ou sommeille,
Qu'un peu de moi-même vermeille,
Vienne à la chair ronde et rebelle!

J'ai grand besoin d'un prompt tourment:
Un mal vif et bien terminé
Vaut mieux qu'un supplice dormant!

Soit donc mon sens illuminé
Par cette infime alerte d'or
Sans qui l'Amour meurt ou s'endort!

48

THE BEE

to Francis de Miomandre

Whatever, and how fine, how fell,
Your barb may feel, my blond bee,
I've just a lacy reverie
Thrown on my tender basket's dell.

a doily
a webbish dream

The bosom's lovely gourd sting well,
Where Love lies dead or sleepily,
To bring some rosy bit of me
To the round flesh's rebel swell!

I need so much a sharp attack:
A vivid hurt, and definite,
Is better than this sleeping rack!

blissful boredom overruled
the waspish overwhelm
the drooled.

So may my sense again be lit
By that slight golden warning's rise,
For without that Love sleeps or dies!

POÉSIE

Par la surprise saisie,
Une bouche qui buvait
Au sein de la Poésie
En sépare son duvet:

– O ma mère Intelligence,
De qui la douceur coulait,
Quelle est cette négligence
Qui laisse tarir son lait!

A peine sur ta poitrine,
Accablé de blancs liens,
Me berçait l'onde marine
De ton cœur chargé de biens;

A peine, dans ton ciel sombre,
Abattu sur ta beauté,
Je sentais, à boire l'ombre,
M'envahir une clarté!

Dieu perdu dans son essence,
Et délicieusement
Docile à la connaissance
Du suprême apaisement,

Je touchais à la nuit pure,
Je ne savais plus mourir,
Car un fleuve sans coupure
Me semblait me parcourir...

POETRY

Foiled unexpectedly,
A mouth that had been feeding,
Suckled by Poetry,
Parted its down in pleading:

'O Mother Intelligence
Whose sweetness used to pour,
What is this negligence
That stops your milk once more!

'Seldom upon your breast
In the white bonds immersed
Did your goodness rest
Me on your sea-swell nursed;

'Seldom in your sky, grey
On your beauty weighed,
I felt, to drink away
The shade, a light invade!

'A god lost in his essence,
And with delight extreme,
Open to conscious presence
Of appeasement supreme,

'I touched on pure night,
Death I knew no more:
I sensed a river right
Through me endless pour ...

Dis, par quelle crainte vaine,
Par quelle ombre de dépit,
Cette merveilleuse veine
A mes lèvres se rompit?

O rigueur, tu m'es un signe
Qu'à mon âme je déplus!
Le silence au vol de cygne
Entre nous ne règne plus!

Immortelle, ta paupière
Me refuse mes trésors,
Et la chair s'est faite pierre
Qui fut tendre sous mon corps!

Des cieux même tu me sèvres,
Par quel injuste retour?
Que seras-tu sans mes lèvres?
Que serai-je sans amour?

Mais la Source suspendue
Lui répond sans dureté:
– Si fort vous m'avez mordue
Que mon cœur s'est arrêté!

'Tell me through what vain dread,
Through what shadow of spite,
This marvellous vein that fed
My lips is closed off tight?

'A sign to me, harsh plight,
That I've displeased my soul!
Silence in the swan's flight
Between us no longer whole!

'Immortal Goddess, your lids
Deny me now my treasures,
Your flesh turned stone forbids
Mine from its gentle pressures!

'By what unfair eclipse
D'you wean me off that sky?
You're what without my lips?
What without love am I?'

Without asperity
The pending Source replied:
'So hard you've bitten me
You stopped the heart in my side.'

LES PAS

Tes pas, enfants de mon silence,
Saintement, lentement placés,
Vers le lit de ma vigilance
Procèdent muets et glacés.

Personne pure, ombre divine,
Qu'ils sont doux, tes pas retenus!
Dieux!… tous les dons que je devine
Viennent à moi sur ces pieds nus!

Si, de tes lèvres avancées,
Tu prépares pour l'apaiser,
A l'habitant de mes pensées
La nourriture d'un baiser,

Ne hâte pas cet acte tendre,
Douceur d'être et de n'être pas,
Car j'ai vécu de vous attendre
Et mon cœur n'était que vos pas.

THE STEPS

Children of my silence, they tread,
Your steps, saintly, gently, unrushed
Towards the vigil of my bed,
Processional, polished and hushed.

Someone pure, a shadow divine,
Your cautious steps, how sweet, how sweet!
Gods!... All the gifts imagined mine
Come to me on those naked feet!

If, with your lips now forward brought,
You're ready to allay like this
The inhabitant of my thought
With the nourishment of a kiss,

Don't rush the tender action through,
Being and not being, so sweet;
For I have lived awaiting you,
My heart was just your padding feet.

LA CEINTURE

Quand le ciel couleur d'une joue
Laisse enfin les yeux le chérir
Et qu'au point doré de périr
Dans les roses le temps se joue,

Devant le muet de plaisir
Qu'enchaîne une telle peinture,
Danse une Ombre à libre ceinture
Que le soir est près de saisir.

Cette ceinture vagabonde
Fait dans le souffle aérien
Frémir le suprême lien
De mon silence avec ce monde…

Absent, présent… Je suis bien seul,
Et sombre, ô suave linceul.

THE SASH

When sky the colour of a cheek
Allows the sight a cherished eyeing
And on the golden verge of dying
In the roses time plays hide-and-seek,

Before one dumbfound with delight
That such a painting captivates,
With flying sash a Shade gyrates
That evening's close to seize in flight.

In the light breath of air swirled,
That flying sash so vagabond
Sets quivering the final bond
Of my silence with this world...

Absent, present... I'm quite alone,
And sombre, shroud so sweetly sewn.

LA DORMEUSE

à Lucien Fabre.

Quels secrets dans son cœur brûle ma jeune amie,
Ame par le doux masque aspirant une fleur?
De quels vains aliments sa naïve chaleur
Fait ce rayonnement d'une femme endormie?

Souffle, songes, silence, invincible accalmie,
Tu triomphes, ô paix plus puissante qu'un pleur,
Quand de ce plein sommeil l'onde grave et l'ampleur
Conspirent sur le sein d'une telle ennemie.

Dormeuse, amas doré d'ombres et d'abandons,
Ton repos redoutable est chargé de tels dons,
O biche avec langueur longue auprès d'une grappe,

Que malgré l'âme absente, occupée aux enfers,
Ta forme au ventre pur qu'un bras fluide drape,
Veille; ta forme veille, et mes yeux sont ouverts.

THE SLEEPING WOMAN

to Lucien Fabre

What burning secrets does my young friend keep,
Soul breathing through her gentle mask a flower?
What vain foods does this artless warmth devour
To light the radiance of a woman's sleep?

Breath, silence, dreams, calm invincibly deep,
You triumph, peace beyond a tear in power,
When, on the breast of such a foe, the hour
Of sleep's high tide conspires with slow full sweep.

Sleeper, gold mass of shadows, wanton shifts,
Your awesome peace is loaded with such gifts,
Doe in your long languor beside the grapes,

That, though your soul in hells is occupied,
With its clear belly a liquid arm now drapes,
Your form's awake, awake, and my eyes are wide.

FRAGMENTS DU NARCISSE

Cur aliquid vidi?

I

Que tu brilles enfin, terme pur de ma course!

Ce soir, comme d'un cerf, la fuite vers la source
Ne cesse qu'il ne tombe au milieu des roseaux,
Ma soif me vient abattre au bord même des eaux.
Mais, pour désaltérer cette amour curieuse,
Je ne troublerai pas l'onde mystérieuse:
Nymphes! si vous m'aimez, il faut toujours dormir!
La moindre âme dans l'air vous fait toutes frémir;
Même, dans sa faiblesse, aux ombres échappée,
Si la feuille éperdue effleure la napée,
Elle suffit à rompre un univers dormant...
Votre sommeil importe à mon enchantement,
Il craint jusqu'au frisson d'une plume qui plonge!
Gardez-moi longuement ce visage pour songe
Qu'une absence divine est seule à concevoir!
Sommeil des nymphes, ciel, ne cessez de me voir!
Rêvez, rêvez de moi!... Sans vous, belles fontaines,
Ma beauté, ma douleur, me seraient incertaines.
Je chercherais en vain ce que j'ai de plus cher,
Sa tendresse confuse étonnerait ma chair,
Et mes tristes regards, ignorants de mes charmes,
A d'autres que moi-même adresseraient leurs larmes...

Vous attendiez, peut-être, un visage sans pleurs,
Vous calmes, vous toujours de feuilles et de fleurs,
Et de l'incorruptible altitude hantées,

FRAGMENTS OF THE 'NARCISSUS'

Cur aliquid vidi?
(Why have I seen something?)

I

At last you shine, pure end of all my course!

This evening, as if a hind's towards the source,
Ceaseless until it drops into the sedge,
My thirst attacks me at the water's edge.
And yet I'll not disturb the mysterious pool
Just so this curious love be quenched and cool:
Nymphs, if you love me you must never wake!
The least soul in the air will have you quake;
Even in its weakness, from shadows taking flight,
Should lost leaf brush against a water-sprite,
It would disrupt a dormant universe...
Your sleep is vital or my charms disperse.
They fear as much a quivering plume's extreme!
Keep me this face a long time for dream
Divine absence alone conceives to be!
Slumber of nymphs, sky, watch always me!
Dream, dream of me!... Without you, lovely springs,
My beauty, my sorrow would be uncertain things.
I'd seek in vain the dearest I possess,
Its tenderness perturbed would shock my flesh.
My wistful looks, unconscious of my charms,
Would turn their tears from me to other arms...

You'd wait a face without the weeping showers,
Perhaps, you calm, you always of leaves, flowers,
And haunted by the incorruptible height,

O Nymphes!... Mais docile aux pentes enchantées
Qui me firent vers vous d'invincibles chemins,
Souffrez ce beau reflet des désordres humains!

Heureux vos corps fondus, Eaux planes et profondes!
Je suis seul!... Si les Dieux, les échos et les ondes
Et si tant de soupirs permettent qu'on le soit!
Seul!... mais encor celui qui s'approche de soi
Quand il s'approche aux bords que bénit ce feuillage...
Des cimes, l'air déjà cesse le pur pillage;
La voix des sources change, et me parle du soir;
Un grand calme m'écoute, où j'écoute l'espoir.
J'entends l'herbe des nuits croître dans l'ombre sainte,
Et la lune perfide élève son miroir
Jusque dans les secrets de la fontaine éteinte...
Jusque dans les secrets que je crains de savoir,
Jusque dans le repli de l'amour de soi-même,
Rien ne peut échapper au silence du soir...
La nuit vient sur ma chair lui souffler que je l'aime.
Sa voix fraîche à mes vœux tremble de consentir;
A peine, dans la brise, elle semble mentir,
Tant le frémissement de son temple tacite
Conspire au spacieux silence d'un tel site.

O douceur de survivre à la force du jour,
Quand elle se retire enfin rose d'amour,
Encore un peu brûlante, et lasse, mais comblée,
Et de tant de trésors tendrement accablée
Par de tels souvenirs qu'ils empourprent sa mort,
Et qu'ils la font heureuse agenouiller dans l'or,
Puis s'étendre, se fondre, et perdre sa vendange,
Et s'éteindre en un songe en qui le soir se change.

Quelle perte en soi-même offre un si calme lieu!
L'âme, jusqu'à périr, s'y penche pour un Dieu

O Nymphs!... Led by enchanted slopes whose sleight
Drew me by routes compelling to your borders,
Suffer this fine reflection of man's disorders!

Happy your liquid flesh, level profound!
I am alone!... If the Gods, waves, echo's sound,
And if so many sighs will let me be!
Alone!... yet one who nears to self when he
Approaches near these banks blest by the leaves...
The purity from peaks air no more thieves;
The voice of sources changes, speaks evening near;
A great calm hears me where hope I hear.
In holy dark I hear night's growing grass.
The fickle moon lifts up her mirror clear,
Right in the dim pool's secrets leans her glass...
Right in the secrets where I dread to peer,
Right in recesses of self-love's self-covet,
Nothing evades the silence of evening here...
Night on my body comes and breathes I love it.
To my hopes its fresh voice quakes to comply;
Under the breeze it hardly seems to lie,
The tremors of its tacit shrine unite
So well with spacious silence round this site.

What sweetness, living through the prime of day
When in rose of love at last she draws away,
Burning a little still, lazy, fulfilled,
And with such treasure gently quelled, and stilled
By such memories as purple death for her,
And make her happy to kneel in the gold blur,
To loll and melt and lose that gold of grapes
And lull into a dream where evening shapes.

What loss in self so calm a place bespeaks!
The soul, about to die, leans there and seeks

Qu'elle demande à l'onde, onde déserte, et digne
Sur son lustre, du lisse effacement d'un cygne...
    A cette onde jamais ne burent les troupeaux!
D'autres, ici perdus, trouveraient le repos,
Et dans la sombre terre, un clair tombeau qui s'ouvre...
Mais ce n'est pas le calme, hélas! que j'y découvre!
Quand l'opaque délice où dort cette clarté,
Cède à mon corps l'horreur du feuillage écarté,
Alors, vainqueur de l'ombre, ô mon corps tyrannique,
Repoussant aux forêts leur épaisseur panique,
Tu regrettes bientôt leur éternelle nuit!
Pour l'inquiet Narcisse, il n'est ici qu'ennui!
Tout m'appelle et m'enchaîne à la chair lumineuse
Que m'oppose des eaux la paix vertigineuse!

Que je déplore ton éclat fatal et pur,
Si mollement de moi fontaine environnée,
Où puisèrent mes yeux dans un mortel azur,
Les yeux mêmes et noirs de leur âme étonnée.

Profondeur, profondeur, songes qui me voyez,
        Comme ils verraient une autre vie,
Dites, ne suis-je pas celui que vous croyez,
        Votre corps vous fait-il envie?
Cessez, sombres esprits, cet ouvrage anxieux
        Qui se fait dans l'âme qui veille;
Ne cherchez pas en vous, n'allez surprendre aux cieux
        Le malheur d'être une merveille:
Trouvez dans la fontaine un corps délicieux...

Prenant à vos regards cette parfaite proie,
Du monstre de s'aimer faites-vous un captif;
Dans les errants filets de vos longs cils de soie
Son gracieux éclat vous retienne pensif;

A God from water, deserted, deserving on
Its gloss, the sleek effacement of a swan...
    These waters cattle never came to drink!
Others, lost here, would find peace on the brink,
And in the dark earth a clear tomb appear...
It isn't calm, alas, that I find here!
When obscure delight, where sleeps that clarity,
Cedes the horror of foliage spread to me,
Then, victor of the shadow, flesh tyranny,
Routing to forests their Panic density,
Their night's eternity you soon regret!
For restless Narcissus, here's but ennui's net!
All draws and chains me to the flesh that glows
Facing me in the waters' giddying repose.

How I lament your brilliance, fatal, pure,
So softly round me, fount, your water lies,
Where from a deadly blue my eyes procure
Their soul's astonished, dark and selfsame eyes.

Depths, depths, dreams that see me and reflect,
        As if another life looked down,
Tell me, aren't I all that you'd expect,
        And would your body have me drown?
Cease, sombre spirits, cease these anxious rites
        That in the watchful soul are done.
Don't seek within; nor snatch down from the heights
        The fate of being a marvellous one:
Find in the pool a body that delights...

Catching with your looks this perfect prey,
Of monstrous self-love make yourself a capture;
In straying threads of your long silk lashes may
His graceful brilliance hold your pensive rapture;

Mais ne vous flattez pas de le changer d'empire.
　　Ce cristal est son vrai séjour;
　　Les efforts mêmes de l'amour
Ne le sauraient de l'onde extraire qu'il n'expire…

PIRE.
　　Pire?…
　　　　　Quelqu'un redit *Pire*… O moqueur!
Écho lointaine est prompte à rendre son oracle!
De son rire enchanté, le roc brise mon cœur,
　　Et le silence, par miracle,
Cesse!… parle, renaît, sur la face des eaux…
Pire?…
　　　　Pire destin!…Vous le dites, roseaux,
Qui reprîtes des vents ma plainte vagabonde!
Antres, qui me rendez mon âme plus profonde,
Vous renflez de votre ombre une voix qui se meurt…
Vous me le murmurez, ramures!… O rumeur
Déchirante, et docile aux souffles sans figure,
Votre or léger s'agite, et joue avec l'augure…
Tout se mêle de moi, brutes divinités!
Mes secrets dans les airs sonnent ébruités,
Le roc rit; l'arbre pleure; et par sa voix charmante,
Je ne puis jusqu'aux cieux que je ne me lamente
D'appartenir sans force à d'éternels attraits!
Hélas! entre les bras qui naissent des forêts,
Une tendre lueur d'heure ambiguë existe…
Là, d'un reste du jour, se forme un fiancé,
Nu, sur la place pâle où m'attire l'eau triste,
Délicieux démon désirable et glacé!

Te voici, mon doux corps de lune et de rosée,
O forme obéissante à mes vœux opposée!
Qu'ils sont beaux, de mes bras les dons vastes et vains!
Mes lentes mains, dans l'or adorable se lassent

Don't think you'll make him put his kingdom by.
　　　His dwelling is this crystal source;
　　　And love itself knows not the force
To draw him from the pool unless he die...

DIRE.
　　　Dire?...
　　　　　　Dire... repeats some mocker after!
Distant Echo's quick to speak her oracle!
Rock breaks my heart, with her enchanted laughter,
　　　And the silence, like a miracle,
Ceases!... speaks, repeats over the water's edge...
Dire?...
　　　Dire fate!... You say so, sedge,
Taking from winds, my plaint that wanders round!
Caverns that give my soul back more profound,
You're swelling with your shadow a voice that dies...
You boughs murmur it me, ramose sighs...
Harrowing rumour, to faceless breaths amenable,
Your light gold stirs and plays with oracle...
Everything's merged with me, brute deities!
My secrets are dispersed upon the breeze,
Rock laughs; tree weeps; I only have the choice
To mourn myself to the skies by its charming voice
For being powerless part of eternal traits!
Alas, between the arms that forests raise,
Is the ambiguous hour's soft lucency...
There, at day's end, a lover forms and lies
Nude on the pale plane, sad pool drawing me,
Delightful demon, desirable and ice!

You're here, my sweet body of moon and dew,
O form swayed by my hopes, opposite, you!
The vast vain gifts of my arms, how very fine!
My slow hands tire in the adorable gold

D'appeler ce captif que les feuilles enlacent;
Mon cœur jette aux échos l'éclat des noms divins!...

   Mais que ta bouche est belle en ce muet blasphème!
O semblable!... Et pourtant plus parfait que moi-même,
Éphémère immortel, si clair devant mes yeux,
Pâles membres de perle, et ces cheveux soyeux,
Faut-il qu'à peine aimés, l'ombre les obscurcisse,
Et que la nuit déjà nous divise, ô Narcisse,
Et glisse entre nous deux le fer qui coupe un fruit!
Qu'as-tu?
              Ma plainte même est funeste?...
                                    Le bruit
Du souffle que j'enseigne à tes lèvres, mon double,
Sur la limpide lame a fait courir un trouble!...
Tu trembles!... Mais ces mots que j'expire à genoux
Ne sont pourtant qu'une âme hésitante entre nous,
Entre ce front si pur et ma lourde mémoire...
Je suis si près de toi que je pourrais te boire,
O visage!... Ma soif est un esclave nu...
   Jusqu'à ce temps charmant je m'étais inconnu,
Et je ne savais pas me chérir et me joindre!
Mais te voir, cher esclave, obéir à la moindre
Des ombres dans mon cœur se fuyant à regret,
Voir sur mon front l'orage et les feux d'un secret,
Voir, ô merveille, voir! ma bouche nuancée
Trahir... peindre sur l'onde une fleur de pensée,
Et quels événements étinceler dans l'œil!

J'y trouve un tel trésor d'impuissance et d'orgueil,
Que nulle vierge enfant échappée au satyre,
Nulle! aux fuites habile, aux chutes sans émoi,
Nulle des nymphes, nulle amie, ne m'attire
Comme tu fais sur l'onde, inépuisable Moi!...

68

Of calling up this captive leaves enfold;
My heart heaves echoes of the names divine!...

How fine your mouth in blasphemy's mute cry!
My image! Yet more perfect still than I,
Immortal transient, clear before my sight,
Pale teeth of pearl and hair so silken light,
Now just when loved the shadows darken you,
Narcissus, night now splits us into two
And slits us like a fruit beneath the knife!
What's the matter?
                                My plaint's funereal?...
                                                        The strife
Of sighs I send towards your lips, my double,
Upon the limpid foil has stirred some trouble!...
You tremble!... Yet these words I, kneeling, offered
Are just a soul of breath between us hovered,
Between my heavy thoughts and your clear brow...
I'm close enough to you to drink you now,
O face!... A naked slave my thirst must be...
    Till this charming time I was unknown to me,
Not knowing how to love myself, embrace!
But to see you, dear slave, obey all trace
Of shadows in my heart, quick to regret,
To see your brow with secret storms beset,
To see my shadowed mouth, O marvel caught,
Betray... upon the pool a flower of thought,
And in the eyes such instants shining clear!

I find such wealth of pride and impotence here
That not a virgin-child that foiled the satyr,
None used to flight, to fall unmoved, no she,
No girl-friend, nymph, could lure and flatter
As you do, on the pool, unfathomed Me!...

II

Fontaine, ma fontaine, eau froidement présente,
Douce aux purs animaux, aux humains complaisante
Qui d'eux-mêmes tentés suivent au fond la mort,
Tout est songe pour toi, Sœur tranquille du Sort!
A peine en souvenir change-t-il un présage,
Que pareille sans cesse à son fuyant visage,
Sitôt de ton sommeil les cieux te sont ravis!
Mais si pure tu sois des êtres que tu vis,
Onde, sur qui les ans passent comme les nues,
Que de choses pourtant doivent t'être connues,
Astres, roses, saisons, les corps et leurs amours!

    Claire, mais si profonde, une nymphe toujours
Effleurée, et vivant de tout ce qui l'approche,
Nourrit quelque sagesse à l'abri de sa roche,
A l'ombre de ce jour qu'elle peint sous les bois.
Elle sait à jamais les choses d'une fois...

    O présence pensive, eau calme qui recueilles
Tout un sombre trésor de fables et de feuilles,
L'oiseau mort, le fruit mûr, lentement descendus,
Et les rares lueurs des clairs anneaux perdus.
Tu consommes en toi leur perte solennelle;
Mais, sur la pureté de ta face éternelle,
L'amour passe et périt...

                    Quand le feuillage épars
Tremble, commence à fuir, pleure de toutes parts,
Tu vois du sombre amour s'y mêler la tourmente,
L'amant brûlant et dur ceindre la blanche amante,
Vaincre l'âme... Et tu sais selon quelle douceur
Sa main puissante passe à travers l'épaisseur
Des tresses que répand la nuque précieuse,
S'y repose, et se sent forte et mystérieuse;
Elle parle à l'épaule et règne sur la chair.

II

Pool, O my pool, water coldly present,
Fresh to pure beasts, to humans acquiescent,
Who tempted in themselves reach death's extreme,
Fate's tranquil Sister, all, for you, is dream!
A presage scarcely turns to memory's trace
Than, as unceasingly, your fleeing face,
So from your sleep the skies are reft from you!
But, pool, if you're unmarked by beings you view,
Where years pass over you as clouds have flown,
What hoards of things indeed you must have known,
Stars, roses, seasons, bodies and their love!

Clear but profound, a nymph, skimmed above
Always, and live to all who near her zone,
Nurtures some wisdom in her shelter of stone,
In shadows of this light she paints under trees.
She knows forever what a moment sees...

O pensive presence, calm pool that receives
All of the sombre trove of fables, leaves,
The dying bird, ripe fruits that gently fall,
Rare gleams of fairest rings beyond recall.
You swallow in yourself their solemn loss;
But there upon your pure eternal gloss,
Love passes, dies...
              When sparse foliage creeps,
Shakes, starts to fly, and everywhere it weeps,
You watch the mingled grief of sombre love,
The lover, burning fierce for his white dove,
Conquer the soul... And know the gentleness
With which his strong hand stirs each heavy tress
The precious nape spreads out along its length;
It rests there, feeling mystery and strength;
Speaks to the shoulder, and on the flesh holds sway.

Alors les yeux fermés à l'éternel éther
Ne voient plus que le sang qui dore leurs paupières;
Sa pourpre redoutable obscurcit les lumières
D'un couple aux pieds confus qui se mêle, et se ment.
Ils gémissent... La Terre appelle doucement
Ces grands corps chancelants, qui luttent bouche à bouche,
Et qui, du vierge sable osant battre la couche,
Composeront d'amour un monstre qui se meurt...
Leurs souffles ne font plus qu'une heureuse rumeur,
L'âme croit respirer l'âme toute prochaine,
Mais tu sais mieux que moi, vénérable fontaine,
Quels fruits forment toujours ces moments enchantés!

     Car, à peine les cœurs calmes et contentés
D'une ardente alliance expirée en délices,
Des amants détachés tu mires les malices,
Tu vois poindre des jours de mensonges tissus,
Et naître mille maux trop tendrement conçus!

     Bientôt, mon onde sage, infidèle et la même,
Le Temps mène ces fous qui crurent que l'on aime
Redire à tes roseaux de plus profonds soupirs!
Vers toi, leurs tristes pas suivent leurs souvenirs...

     Sur tes bords, accablés d'ombres et de faiblesse,
Tout éblouis d'un ciel dont la beauté les blesse
Tant il garde l'éclat de leurs jours les plus beaux,
Ils vont des biens perdus trouver tous les tombeaux...
«Cette place dans l'ombre était tranquille et nôtre!»
«L'autre aimait ce cyprès, se dit le cœur de l'autre,
«Et d'ici, nous goûtions le souffle de la mer!»
Hélas! la rose même est amère dans l'air...
Moins amers les parfums des suprêmes fumées
Qu'abandonnent au vent les feuilles consumées!...

     Ils respirent ce vent, marchent sans le savoir,
Foulent aux pieds le temps d'un jour de désespoir...
O marche lente, prompte, et pareille aux pensées
Qui parlent tour à tour aux têtes insensées!

Then, eyes closed to the eternal ether, they
See just the blood that tints their lids with gold;
Its dauntless red obscures the lights twofold
Of a pair that join, feet mixed, exchanging lies.
They groan ... Gently for them the Earth sighs,
Fine figures, mouth to mouth, and hand to hand,
Who, daring to pound the couch of virgin sand,
Will make of love a monster that is dying ...
Their breaths do no more than a happy sighing,
Soul thinks to breathe the soul that presses near,
Though, hallowed fountain, you know better here
What fruits succeed these spells so full of charm!

For scarcely are the hearts content and calm
From burning union, exhausted with delight,
The lovers loose, than you observe their spite,
You see the dawn of webs of thin deceit,
A thousand evils, born too soft and sweet!

And soon, my good pool, faithless and staunch,
Time leads these fools to think they'd like to launch
Their deepest sighs again among your reeds!
To you their saddened trail of memory leads ...

Shackled with frailties, shadows on your shore,
Dazzled with skies whose beauty wounds them more
So clear they keep the gloss of days once fair,
They'll find the tomb of their well-being there ...
'Once ours and calm, this nook that shadows cover!'
'The other loved this cypress,' mused one lover,
'From here we savoured breaths from off the seas.'
Even the rose is bitter on the breeze ...
Less bitter is the final reek that's thinned
From the burnt leaves and left along the wind! ...

They breathe this wind, walk without knowing where,
Crush underfoot time of a day of despair ...
O slow march, hasty, like thought on thought
That murmurs turn for turn in minds distraught!

La caresse et le meurtre hésitent dans leurs mains,
Leur cœur, qui croit se rompre au détour des chemins,
Lutte, et retient à soi son espérance étreinte.
Mais leurs esprits perdus courent ce labyrinthe
Où s'égare celui qui maudit le soleil!
Leur folle solitude, à l'égal du sommeil,
Peuple et trompe l'absence; et leur secrète oreille
Partout place une voix qui n'a point de pareille...
Rien ne peut dissiper leurs songes absolus;
Le soleil ne peut rien contre ce qui n'est plus!
Mais s'ils traînent dans l'or leurs yeux secs et funèbres,
Ils se sentent des pleurs défendre leurs ténèbres
Plus chères à jamais que tous les feux du jour!
Et dans ce corps caché tout marqué de l'amour,
Que porte amèrement l'âme qui fut heureuse
Brûle un secret baiser qui la rend furieuse...

Mais moi, Narcisse aimé, je ne suis curieux
      Que de ma seule essence;
Tout autre n'a pour moi qu'un cœur mystérieux,
      Tout autre n'est qu'absence.
O mon bien souverain, cher corps, je n'ai que toi!
Le plus beau des mortels ne peut chérir que soi...
   Douce et dorée, est-il une idole plus sainte,
De toute une forêt qui se consume, ceinte,
Et sise dans l'azur, vivant par tant d'oiseaux?
Est-il don plus divin de la faveur des eaux,
Et d'un jour qui se meurt plus adorable usage
Que de rendre à mes yeux l'honneur de mon visage?
Naisse donc entre nous que la lumière unit
De grâce et de silence un échange infini!

   Je vous salue, enfant de mon âme et de l'onde,
Cher trésor d'un miroir qui partage le monde!
Ma tendresse y vient boire, et s'enivre de voir
Un désir sur soi-même essayer son pouvoir!

Caress and murder dither from hand to fist,
Their heart that hopes to break on paths that twist,
Struggles and holds within its slender hope.
But in this labyrinth their lost spirits lope
Where he who execrates the sun's astray!
Their foolish solitude, as in sleep's way,
Peoples and deludes absence; their inner ear
Catches a matchless voice anywhere here...
Their absolute dreams nothing can dismiss;
The sun do nought with what no longer is!
But, should they drag their dry funereal eyes
Into the gold, protective tears will rise
To guard their glooms dearer than light above!
And, hidden in this body marked by love
That bears in bitterness the soul once glad,
Kindles a secret kiss that drives them mad...

Loved Narcissus, there's just this drive in me:
      My own essence I must find;
Any other's but a heart of mystery,
      Any other's absence to my mind.
O my liege lord, dear flesh, I have but you!
Love self is all the loveliest man could do...
   Is there an image more holy, gold and soft,
Framed in a forest burning up aloft,
Decked with so many birds in azure's zone?
What's more divine, by water's favour shown,
And by a dying day, more marvellous grace
Than giving my eyes the homage of my face?
May there be born between us whom light blends
Exchange of grace and silence that never ends!
   Child of my soul and the pool, I welcome you,
Treasure of a glass that splits the world in two!
My love's here to imbibe till drunk in seeing
Desire attempt its power on its own being!

O qu'à tous mes souhaits, que vous êtes semblable!
Mais la fragilité vous fait inviolable,
Vous n'êtes que lumière, adorable moitié
D'une amour trop pareille à la faible amitié!
    Hélas! la nymphe même a séparé nos charmes!
Puis-je espérer de toi que de vaines alarmes?
Qu'ils sont doux les périls que nous pourrions choisir!
Se surprendre soi-même et soi-même saisir,
Nos mains s'entremêler, nos maux s'entredétruire,
Nos silences longtemps de leurs songes s'instruire,
La même nuit en pleurs confondre nos yeux clos,
Et nos bras refermés sur les mêmes sanglots
Étreindre un même cœur, d'amour prêt à se fondre...
    Quitte enfin le silence, ose enfin me répondre,
Bel et cruel Narcisse, inaccessible enfant,
Tout orné de mes biens que la nymphe défend...

Oh, how identical to all I hope!
But frailty keeps you safe beyond my scope,
You're only light, adorable half an affair
Too much akin to friendship's weakness there!

    Alas! the nymph herself has split our charms!
Could I expect much more than false alarms?
How sweet the risks that we ourselves could take!
The self surprising self, seizing its sake,
Our hands entwining, our ills all co-destroyed,
Our silence with our dreaming self-enjoyed,
The same night mingling in our eyes with sobs,
The same arms comforting the selfsame throbs
That strain one heart, ready in love to blend…

    Dare to reply at last, the silence end,
Lovely and cruel Narcissus that never yields,
Adorned with all my graces that the nymph shields…

III

... Ce corps si pur, sait-il qu'il me puisse séduire?
De quelle profondeur songes-tu de m'instruire,
Habitant de l'abîme, hôte si spécieux
D'un ciel sombre ici-bas précipité des cieux?...
    O le frais ornement de ma triste tendance
Qu'un sourire si proche, et plein de confidence,
Et qui prête à ma lèvre une ombre de danger
Jusqu'à me faire craindre un désir étranger!
Quel souffle vient à l'onde offrir ta froide rose?...
J'aime... *J'aime!*... Et qui donc peut aimer autre chose
Que soi-même?...
                        Toi seul, ô mon corps, mon cher corps,
Je t'aime, unique objet qui me défends des morts!

. . . .

Formons, toi sur ma lèvre, et moi, dans mon silence,
Une prière aux dieux qu'émus de tant d'amour
Sur sa pente de pourpre ils arrêtent le jour!...
Faites, Maîtres heureux, Pères des justes fraudes,
Dites qu'une lueur de rose ou d'émeraudes
Que des songes du soir votre sceptre reprit,
Pure, et toute pareille au plus pur de l'esprit,
Attende, au sein des cieux, que tu vives et veuilles,
Près de moi, mon amour, choisir un lit de feuilles,
Sortir tremblant du flanc de la nymphe au cœur froid,
Et sans quitter mes yeux, sans cesser d'être moi,
Tendre ta forme fraîche, et cette claire écorce...
Oh! te saisir enfin!... Prendre ce calme torse
Plus pur que d'une femme et non formé de fruits...
Mais, d'une pierre simple est le temple où je suis,
Où je vis... Car je vis sur tes lèvres avares!...
    O mon corps, mon cher corps, temple qui me sépares
De ma divinité, je voudrais apaiser

III

… Does this pure form know it could be my seduction?
What depths do you muse of making my instruction,
Dweller in the abyss, alluring guest
Of sombre sky cast down from heaven's crest?…
   Oh, fresh adornment of my wistful leaning,
That a smile so close and full of secret meaning,
And one which lends my lips a shade of danger,
Enough to make me fear desire much stranger!
What breath comes offering the pool your chill rose?…
I love… I love!… And whose love could repose
In aught but self?…
               I love you, you alone,
Dear flesh, my one guard from the dead, my own!

. . . .

Let's make, you on my lips, in silence, me,
Prayers to the gods that moved by such a love
They hold the day's declining red above!…
Act, happy Masters, Sires of just deceit,
Speak that a gleam of rose or green repeat,
Pure as the purest of the spirit gleams,
Reclaimed by Your sceptre from the evening dreams,
Pause in the sky, so that thou live and choose,
Beside me, love, a bed of leaves to use,
Tremblingly quit the heartless nymph's cold thighs,
And me unceasingly, nor leaving my eyes,
Offer your fresh form and that lucent skin…
To hold you, oh, at last!… Your calm flesh win,
Purer than woman's, fruits so fugitive…
But of plain stone the temple where I live,
Where I am…. For I live on your mean lips!…
   Body of mine, my precious, temple that rips
Me from my divinity, I'd like to press

Votre bouche... Et bientôt, je briserais, baiser,
Ce peu qui nous défend de l'extrême existence,
Cette tremblante, frêle, et pieuse distance
Entre moi-même et l'onde, et mon âme, et les dieux!...
    Adieu... Sens-tu frémir mille flottants adieux?
Bientôt va frissonner le désordre des ombres!
L'arbre aveugle vers l'arbre étend ses membres sombres,
Et cherche affreusement l'arbre qui disparaît...
Mon âme ainsi se perd dans sa propre forêt,
Où la puissance échappe à ses formes suprêmes...
L'âme, l'âme aux yeux noirs, touche aux ténèbres mêmes,
Elle se fait immense et ne rencontre rien...
Entre la mort et soi, quel regard est le sien!

    Dieux! de l'auguste jour, le pâle et tendre reste
Va des jours consumés joindre le sort funeste;
Il s'abîme aux enfers du profond souvenir!
Hélas! corps misérable, il est temps de s'unir...
Penche-toi... Baise-toi. Tremble de tout ton être!
L'insaisissable amour que tu me vins promettre
Passe, et dans un frisson, brise Narcisse, et fuit...

Your mouth ... And instantly I'd breach, caress,
This bit that keeps us from extreme existence,
This quivering, this frail and pious distance
Between the pool and me, gods and my soul! ...
   Farewell ... do you sense a thousand farewells shoal?
Go soon to thrill disorder in the shadow glooms!
Blind tree to tree holds out its limbs and looms,
In dreadening search for the tree that vanishes ...
My soul is lost like that, in its own forest is,
Where power the highest of its forms evades ...
The soul, dark-eyed, confronts the same black shades,
Becomes immense and nothing experiences ...
Between death and self, what a sight hers is!

   Gods, how the pale soft end of a day august
Joins in the baneful fate of days turned dust;
It plummets into memory's deepest hell!
Alas! poor flesh, it's time we blend as well ...
Lean over ... Kiss. Tremble with all your soul!
That love, ungraspable, you'd promised whole,
Passes and, shuddering, breaks Narcissus, flees ...

LA PYTHIE

à Pierre Louÿs.

La Pythie exhalant la flamme
De naseaux durcis par l'encens,
Haletante, ivre, hurle!... l'âme
Affreuse, et les flancs mugissants!
Pâle, profondément mordue,
Et la prunelle suspendue
Au point le plus haut de l'horreur,
Le regard qui manque à son masque
S'arrache vivant à la vasque,
A la fumée, à la fureur!

Sur le mur, son ombre démente
Où domine un démon majeur,
Parmi l'odorante tourmente
Prodigue un fantôme nageur,
De qui la transe colossale,
Rompant les aplombs de la salle,
Si la folle tarde à hennir,
Mime de noirs enthousiasmes,
Hâte les dieux, presse les spasmes
De s'achever dans l'avenir!

Cette martyre en sueurs froides,
Ses doigts sur mes doigts se crispant,
Vocifère entre les ruades
D'un trépied qu'étrangle un serpent:
– Ah! maudite!... Quels maux je souffre!
Toute ma nature est un gouffre!
Hélas! Entr'ouverte aux esprits,
J'ai perdu mon propre mystère!...

THE PYTHONESS

to Pierre Louÿs

The Pythoness, exhaling flame,
From incense-hardened nostril-holes,
Is howling, drunk and gasping!... Her frame
Shakes with bellows, and her soul's
Fearful! Pale, profoundly possessed,
Her eyeballs in suspense, oppressed
At the peak of horror's height,
And, vacant in her mask, her gaze
Wrenches itself from cresset-blaze
To the smoke, to frenzy's flight!

Across the wall her shadow insane,
That a superior demon subdues
Amid the aromatic pain,
Casts a phantom swimmer whose
Colossal trance, breaking the hall's
Perpendiculars as it sprawls,
If the mad woman's slow to neigh,
Mimics some dark enthusiasms,
Hastens the gods, speeds up the spasms
To end upon the future's say!

This martyr, in her cold sweat,
Her fingers in my fingers pokes,
Gives voice between the buck and jet
Of a tripod that a serpent chokes:
'Ah, cursed!... What ills I bear in this!
My whole nature is an abyss!
Alas! To spirits a loophole,
The mystery of myself I've lost!...

Une Intelligence adultère
Exerce un corps qu'elle a compris!

Don cruel! Maître immonde, cesse
Vite, vite, ô divin ferment,
De feindre une vaine grossesse
Dans ce pur ventre sans amant!
Fais finir cette horrible scène!
Vois de tout mon corps l'arc obscène
Tendre à se rompre pour darder
Comme son trait le plus infâme,
Implacablement au ciel l'âme
Que mon sein ne peut plus garder!

Qui me parle, à ma place même?
Quel écho me répond: Tu mens!
Qui m'illumine?... Qui blasphème?
Et qui, de ces mots écumants,
Dont les éclats hachent ma langue,
La fait brandir une harangue
Brisant la bave et les cheveux
Que mâche et trame le désordre
D'une bouche qui veut se mordre
Et se reprendre ses aveux?

Dieu! Je ne me connais de crime
Que d'avoir à peine vécu!...
Mais si tu me prends pour victime
Et sur l'autel d'un corps vaincu
Si tu courbes un monstre, tue
Ce monstre, et la bête abattue,
Le col tranché, le chef produit
Par les crins qui tirent les tempes,
Que cette plus pâle des lampes
Saisisse de marbre la nuit!

An adulterous Intellect's crossed,
And works a body in its control!

'Cruel gift! Disgusting master, end,
Swiftly, swiftly, O ferment divine,
The false pregnancy you pretend
In this unloved virgin womb of mine!
Finish the horror of this scene!
My whole body, obscene, unclean,
Look, arched to breaking point to train
At heaven that arrow most ill-famed,
The soul, inexorably aimed,
My breast no longer can retain!

'Who in my own place speaks to me?
What echo answers me: You liar!
Who enlightens me?... Whose blasphemy?
Who, with these foaming words whose dire
Outbursts hash my utterance, makes
It lash out some harangue that breaks
Through drool and the dishevelled hair,
Twisted and chewed by a mouth confused
That wishes to repent, misused,
And all the vows it made unswear?

'God! I admit only the vice
Of scarcely having lived!... If now
You take me as a sacrifice
And if you make a monster bow
On the vanquished body's altar, slay
That monster, and, carcase cast away,
The neck severed, temples drawn tight
By its grasped hair, display the head
So that this palest light be shed
And into marble turn the night!

Alors, par cette vagabonde
Morte, errante, et lune à jamais,
Soit l'eau des mers surprise, et l'onde
Astreinte à d'éternels sommets!
Que soient les humains faits statues,
Les cœurs figés, les âmes tues,
Et par les glaces de mon œil,
Puisse un peuple de leurs paroles
Durcir en un peuple d'idoles
Muet de sottise et d'orgueil!

Eh! Quoi… Devenir la vipère
Dont tout le ressort de frissons
Surprend la chair que désespère
Sa multitude de tronçons!…
Reprendre une lutte insensée!…
Tourne donc plutôt ta pensée
Vers la joie enfuie, et reviens,
O mémoire, à cette magie
Qui ne tirait son énergie
D'autres arcanes que des tiens!

Mon cher corps… Forme préférée,
Fraîcheur par qui ne fut jamais
Aphrodite désaltérée,
Intacte nuit, tendres sommets,
Et vos partages indicibles
D'une argile en îles sensibles,
Douce matière de mon sort,
Quelle alliance nous vécûmes,
Avant que le don des écumes
Ait fait de toi ce corps de mort!

'Then, by this dead wanderer, roaming
And moon forever, let the seas
Be taken by surprise, and foaming
Waves in eternal cresting freeze!
And statuary let men become,
Their hearts congealed, their souls dumb,
And, through my staring icy-eyed,
May a people of their word
Harden to one of idols, absurd,
Mute in stupidity and pride!

'Eh! What, then... Become the snake
Whose shuddering of sensations
Assaults the flesh till it would break
From its multiple articulations!...
Start up again the senseless war!...
No, rather turn your thought once more
Towards the joys that long have flown,
That magic find, O memory,
Magic that draws its energy
From secrets only of your own!

'My dear body... Form chosen first,
Freshness that never quenched the lips
Of Aphrodite in her thirst,
Night perfect, gentle crests and dips,
Those shares, beyond all words and styles,
In that clay of the sensible isles,
What union had we given breath,
Soft material of my fate,
Before the gift, in foaming spate,
Made of you this body of death!

Toi, mon épaule, où l'or se joue
D'une fontaine de noirceur,
J'aimais de te joindre ma joue
Fondue à sa même douceur!...
Ou, soulevée à mes narines,
Ouverte aux distances marines,
Les mains pleines de seins vivants,
Entre mes bras aux belles anses
Mon abîme a bu les immenses
Profondeurs qu'apportent les vents!

Hélas! ô roses, toute lyre
Contient la modulation!
Un soir, de mon triste délire
Parut la constellation!
Le temple se change dans l'antre,
Et l'ouragan des songes entre
Au même ciel qui fut si beau!
Il faut gémir, il faut atteindre
Je ne sais quelle extase, et ceindre
Ma chevelure d'un lambeau!

Ils m'ont connue aux bleus stigmates
Apparus sur ma pauvre peau;
Ils m'assoupirent d'aromates
Laineux et doux comme un troupeau;
Ils ont, pour vivante amulette,
Touché ma gorge qui halète
Sous les ornements vipérins;
Étourdie, ivre d'empyreumes,
Ils m'ont, au murmure des neumes,
Rendu des honneurs souterrains.

'You, O my shoulder, you I used
To like my cheek to join, where gold
Teases a fount of darkness, suffused
In that same softness sweetly lolled!...
Or, raised up to my nose, respond
To ocean distances beyond,
With living breasts my hands full,
Within my arms, lovely and round,
My void has tasted the profound
Heights carried on the wind's pull!

'Alas! O roses, all lyres contain
The modulation! And one night,
From my sad frenzy in the fane,
The constellation rose in sight!
The temple changed into a cave,
The hurricane of dreams to rave
In the same sky that was so fine!
It must be groans; must be attain
Some ecstasy or other; restrain
My tresses in some rag or twine!

'They've known me by stigmata shown
In blue upon my wretched skin;
Doped me with aromatics blown,
Woolly and softly flocking in;
They have, for living amulet,
Fingered my throat gasping to get
Its breath in viper jewelry;
Numbing me drunk on empyreumes,
Have, to the murmuring of neumes,
Subterranean honours rendered me.

Qu'ai-je donc fait qui me condamne
Pure, à ces rites odieux?
Une sombre carcasse d'âne
Eût bien servi de ruche aux dieux!
Mais une vierge consacrée,
Une conque neuve et nacrée
Ne doit à la divinité
Que sacrifice et que silence,
Et cette intime violence
Que se fait la virginité!

Pourquoi, Puissance Créatrice,
Auteur du mystère animal,
Dans cette vierge pour matrice,
Semer les merveilles du mal?
Sont-ce les dons que tu m'accordes?
Crois-tu, quand se brisent les cordes
Que le son jaillisse plus beau?
Ton plectre a frappé sur mon torse,
Mais tu ne lui laisses la force
Que de sonner comme un tombeau!

Sois clémente, sois sans oracles!
Et de tes merveilleuses mains,
Change en caresses les miracles,
Retiens les présents surhumains.
C'est en vain que tu communiques
A nos faibles tiges, d'uniques
Commotions de ta splendeur!
L'eau tranquille est plus transparente
Que toute tempête parente
D'une confuse profondeur!

'But what, then, have I done, alas,
That dooms me, pure, to hateful rites?
The sombre carcase of some ass
As hive for gods well serves its lights!
But a consecrated virgin-girl,
A fresh conch of nacreous pearl
Owes the divine the offering
Only of sacrifice and silence,
And of that intimate violence
Which virginity will bring!

'Why, Creator Power, Source
Of the living mystery, inhume
And sow marvels of evil force
Within this virgin as a womb?
Do you give these gifts to me as apt?
Or think that once the strings are snapped
Lovelier sounds will leap and bloom?
Your plectrum plucked my torso length
And yet you leave it no more strength
Than this, of sounding like a tomb!

'Be merciful, no oracles!
Allow your wondrous hands to act,
To caresses change the miracles,
The superhuman gifts retract.
It is in vain that you should speak
To our frail tendrils these unique
Commotions that your splendour sweeps!
For calm waters are more clear
Than any tempests that may rear
Flaunting confusions of the deeps!

Va, la lumière, la divine
N'est pas l'épouvantable éclair
Qui nous devance et nous devine
Comme un songe cruel et clair!
Il éclate!... Il va nous instruire!...
Non!... La solitude vient luire
Dans la plaie immense des airs
Où nulle pâle architecture,
Mais la déchirante rupture
Nous imprime de purs déserts!

N'allez donc, mains universelles,
Tirer de mon front orageux
Quelques suprêmes étincelles!
Les hasards font les mêmes jeux!
Le passé, l'avenir sont frères
Et par leurs visages contraires
Une seule tête pâlit
De ne voir où qu'elle regarde
Qu'une même absence hagarde
D'îles plus belles que l'oubli.

Noirs témoins de tant de lumières
Ne cherchez plus... Pleurez, mes yeux!...
O pleurs dont les sources premières
Sont trop profondes dans les cieux!...
Jamais plus amère demande!...
Mais la prunelle la plus grande
De ténèbres se doit nourrir!...
Tenant notre race atterrée,
La distance désespérée
Nous laisse le temps de mourir!

'Indeed, the light that is divine
Is not this lightning casting fear
That forestalls, foretells our line,
Like a dream both cruel and clear!
It bursts!... It means to teach us!... No!...
Solitude comes, a brightening glow
In the immense wide wound of the air
Where no wan architecture's hue
But that deep rupture, searing through,
Imprints us with pure deserts there!

'Don't try, then, universal hands,
To strike out of my storm-tossed brow
Supreme sparks from burning brands!
Chance plays the same games anyhow!
Brothers are future and the past;
Opposite ways their eyes are cast.
A single head grows pale as cotton,
Seeing, in either way they stare,
Only the same wild absence there
Of fairer isles than the forgotten.

'Dark witnesses of so many torches
No further search... Weep, weep, eyes!...
O tears whose primary sources
Are too sublime within the skies!...
Never more bitter plea!... Yet still
The greatest eye demands its fill
Of tenebrous glooms and mystifying!...
In earthbound thrall keeping our race,
The desperate distance that we face
Just leaves us with the time for dying!

Entends, mon âme, entends ces fleuves!
Quelles cavernes sont ici?
Est-ce mon sang?... Sont-ce les neuves
Rumeurs des ondes sans merci?
Mes secrets sonnent leurs aurores!
Tristes airains, tempes sonores,
Que dites-vous de l'avenir!
Frappez, frappez, dans une roche,
Abattez l'heure la plus proche...
Mes deux natures vont s'unir!

O formidablement gravie,
Et sur d'effrayants échelons,
Je sens dans l'arbre de ma vie
La mort monter de mes talons!
Le long de ma ligne frileuse,
Le doigt mouillé de la fileuse
Trace une atroce volonté!
Et par sanglots grimpe la crise
Jusque dans ma nuque où se brise
Une cime de volupté!

Ah! brise les portes vivantes!
Fais craquer les vains scellements,
Épais troupeau des épouvantes,
Hérissé d'étincellements!
Surgis des étables funèbres
Où te nourrissaient mes ténèbres
De leur fabuleuse foison!
Bondis, de rêves trop repue,
O horde épineuse et crépue,
Et viens fumer dans l'or, Toison!

'Hark! hark, my soul; these rivers pour!
And whatever are these caves?
Is this my blood?... And are these more
Surges of ruthless, breaking waves?
My secrets their auroras sound!
Sad bronzes, temples that resound,
What of the future do you recite!
Strike at a rock, strike at a rock,
Now, at the present hour, knock...
My two natures will soon unite!

'Oh fearfully scaled, this ledge,
By such precarious holds, I feel
In my living trunk the knife-edge
Of death is rising from my heel!
The full length of my freezing line,
The moist finger that spins the twine
Traces an atrocious will!
Through sobs the mounting crisis makes
Towards my nape until there breaks
Sensuously the summit's thrill!

'The living doors, oh, burst them wide!
Crack the pointless seals apart,
Dense herd of dreads and terrors, stride,
With coats on which the sparkles dart!
Surge from the deathly stables where
My shadows fed you on their fare
Of fabled plentiful increase!
Gambol, with dreams too cloyed and full,
O horde, with spiky tousled wool,
Come steaming in the gold, O Fleece!'

Telle, toujours plus tourmentée,
Déraisonne, râle et rugit
La prophétesse fomentée
Par les souffles de l'or rougi.
Mais enfin le ciel se déclare!
L'oreille du pontife hilare
S'aventure vers le futur:
Une attente sainte la penche,
Car une voix nouvelle et blanche
Échappe de ce corps impur:

Honneur des Hommes, Saint LANGAGE,
Discours prophétique et paré,
Belles chaînes en qui s'engage
Le dieu dans la chair égaré,
Illumination, largesse!
Voici parler une Sagesse
Et sonner cette auguste Voix
Qui se connaît quand elle sonne
N'être plus la voix de personne
Tant que des ondes et des bois!

Thus, tormented more and more,
The prophetess loses her head,
Rails, raves, fomented to the core
By wafts of gold wine-tinctured red.
The heavens declare themselves at last!
The gleeful pontiff's ear has cast
Itself upon futurity:
A holy expectation makes it lean
Because a voice comes fresh and clean
From this impure body, broken free:

Honour of Men, O sacred SPEECH,
Prophetic, ornate discourse, mesh
Of lovely fetters in whose reach
God lost himself and became flesh,
Illumination and largesse!
To speak a Wisdom here, express
That august Voice that's understood
When it resounds to be not voice
So much of any person's choice
But voice of waters and of wood!

LE SYLPHE

Ni vu ni connu
Je suis le parfum
Vivant et défunt
Dans le vent venu!

Ni vu ni connu,
Hasard ou génie:
A peine venu
La tâche est finie!

Ni lu ni compris?
Aux meilleurs esprits
Que d'erreurs promises!

Ni vu ni connu,
Le temps d'un sein nu
Entre deux chemises!

THE SYLPH

Not seen, nor known,
I'm perfume spread
Living and dead
By the wind blown!

Not seen, nor known,
Hazard or feat:
Hardly yet shown
The task's complete!

Unread, undelved?
In best minds shelved
What errors certs!

Not known, not seen,
Time bare breasts lean
Between two shirts!

L'INSINUANT

O Courbes, méandre,
Secrets du menteur,
Est-il art plus tendre
Que cette lenteur?

Je sais où je vais,
Je t'y veux conduire,
Mon dessein mauvais
N'est pas de te nuire...

(Quoique souriante
En pleine fierté,
Tant de liberté
La désoriente!)

O Courbes, méandre,
Secrets du menteur,
Je veux faire attendre
Le mot le plus tendre.

THE INSINUANT

O windings, wander,
Liars' secrecies;
What art is fonder
Than this sloth is?

I know where I go;
I'll take you, too;
My bad plan, though,
Not to hurt you...

(Though she's all smiles
In her full pride,
Freedom so wide
Bewilders, beguiles.)

O windings, wander,
Liars' secrecies;
I'll hold back longer
One word, none fonder.

LA FAUSSE MORTE

Humblement, tendrement, sur le tombeau charmant,
      Sur l'insensible monument,
Que d'ombres, d'abandons, et d'amour prodiguée!
      Forme ta grâce fatiguée,
Je meurs, je meurs sur toi, je tombe et je m'abats,

Mais à peine abattu sur le sépulcre bas,
Dont la close étendue aux cendres me convie,
Cette morte apparente, en qui revient la vie,
Frémit, rouvre les yeux, m'illumine et me mord,
Et m'arrache toujours une nouvelle mort
      Plus précieuse que la vie.

THE FALSE DEAD WOMAN

Tenderly, humbly on the charming tomb's extent,
    On the insentient monument,
What shadows, full abandon, lavish desire!
    Her satiate grace creates, I expire,
Expire on her, I start to fall, and down I drop,

When scarcely sunk on to the tomb's low top,
Whose sealed extent to ashes would inveigle me,
This woman seeming dead comes back to life and she
Trembles, opens her eyes, enlightens me, she seizes,
And wrests from me always a new death, deceases
    More precious than mere life can be.

ÉBAUCHE D'UN SERPENT

à Henri Ghéon.

Parmi l'arbre, la brise berce
La vipère que je vêtis;
Un sourire, que la dent perce
Et qu'elle éclaire d'appétits,
Sur le Jardin se risque et rôde,
Et mon triangle d'émeraude
Tire sa langue à double fil...
Bête je suis, mais bête aiguë,
De qui le venin quoique vil
Laisse loin la sage ciguë!

Suave est ce temps de plaisance!
Tremblez, mortels! Je suis bien fort
Quand jamais à ma suffisance,
Je bâille à briser le ressort!
La splendeur de l'azur aiguise
Cette guivre qui me déguise
D'animale simplicité;
Venez à moi, race étourdie!
Je suis debout et dégourdie,
Pareille à la nécessité!

Soleil, soleil!... Faute éclatante!
Toi qui masques la mort, Soleil,
Sous l'azur et l'or d'une tente
Où les fleurs tiennent leur conseil;
Par d'impénétrables délices,
Toi, le plus fier de mes complices,
Et de mes pièges le plus haut,
Tu gardes les cœurs de connaître

SKETCH OF A SERPENT

to Henri Ghéon

About the boughs the breeze allays
And lulls the viper I invest;
Pierced by a fang whose glint displays
Its appetites, a smile in quest
Upon the Garden risks its chances.
My emerald triangle advances
Its darting tongue of double thread...
A dumb beast, me, but fly I am;
Though vile, my venom, given its head,
Leaves far behind nice hemlock's dram!

How mild this time of pleasant heat!
Tremble, O mortals! I have the might,
Whenever in my own conceit,
To yawn and snap the springs outright!
The splendour of the azure stirs
The serpent whose disguise confers
An animal simplicity.
Come unto me, you heedless race!
I'm on my toes and nothing base,
Comparable with necessity!

The sun, the sun!... You dazzling fault!
You, Sun, who mask mortality
Under the gold and azure vault
Where flowers keep their secrecy;
You, by unfathomable delight,
Proudest accomplice and the height
Of all my most insidious traps,
You keep all hearts from ever seeing

Que l'univers n'est qu'un défaut
Dans la pureté du Non-être!

Grand Soleil, qui sonnes l'éveil
A l'être, et de feux l'accompagnes,
Toi qui l'enfermes d'un sommeil
Trompeusement peint de campagnes,
Fauteur des fantômes joyeux
Qui rendent sujette des yeux
La présence obscure de l'âme,
Toujours le mensonge m'a plu
Que tu répands sur l'absolu.
O roi des ombres fait de flamme

Verse-moi ta brute chaleur,
Où vient ma paresse glacée
Rêvasser de quelque malheur
Selon ma nature enlacée...
Ce lieu charmant qui vit la chair
Choir et se joindre m'est très cher!
Ma fureur, ici, se fait mûre;
Je la conseille et la recuis,
Je m'écoute, et dans mes circuits,
Ma méditation murmure...

O Vanité! Cause Première!
Celui qui règne dans les Cieux,
D'une voix qui fut la lumière
Ouvrit l'univers spacieux.
Comme las de son pur spectacle,
Dieu lui-même a rompu l'obstacle
De sa parfaite éternité;
Il se fit Celui qui dissipe
En conséquences, son Principe,
En étoiles, son Unité.

The universe is just a lapse
In the purity of Non-being!

Great Sun, you whose alarm so rings
For Being, who follow up with heat,
Then close it in a sleep that brings
The landscapes painted with deceit,
Feigner of joyful phantoms there
That render visible in air
The dubious presence of the soul,
I'm always pleased the way you shoot
The lie about the Absolute.
O flame-made King of shadows, dole

Your brute warmth out all over me,
Whereby my icy indolence
Can daydream some calamity
Matching my nature's tortuous sense ...
I like this place that sees the flesh
Flash and then together thresh!
My fury mellows here until
I reason with it, keep it warm,
I hear myself; in circling form
My meditation murmurs still ...

O Vanity! O Thou First Cause!
Thou that rulest Heav'n as Lord,
Whose voice created light, whose laws
Spread worlds of space. Now, as if bored
Of pure spectacle all his own,
God has himself breached through the zone
Of perfect sempiternity;
Creates himself the One who thins
Intent to consequences, spins
His Essence out so starrily.

Cieux, son erreur! Temps, sa ruine!
Et l'abîme animal, béant!...
Quelle chute dans l'origine
Étincelle au lieu de néant!...
Mais, le premier mot de son Verbe,
MOI!... Des astres le plus superbe
Qu'ait parlés le fou créateur,
Je suis!... Je serai!... J'illumine
La diminution divine
De tous les feux du Séducteur!

Objet radieux de ma haine,
Vous que j'aimais éperdument,
Vous qui dûtes de la géhenne
Donner l'empire à cet amant,
Regardez-vous dans ma ténèbre!
Devant votre image funèbre,
Orgueil de mon sombre miroir,
Si profond fut votre malaise
Que votre souffle sur la glaise
Fut un soupir de désespoir!

En vain, Vous avez, dans la fange,
Pétri de faciles enfants,
Qui de Vos actes triomphants
Tout le jour Vous fissent louange!
Sitôt pétris, sitôt soufflés,
Maître Serpent les a sifflés,
Les beaux enfants que Vous créâtes!
Holà! dit-il, nouveaux venus!
Vous êtes des hommes tout nus,
O bêtes blanches et béates!

Skies are his error! His ruin, Time!
The bestial abyss that gapes so base!...
O what a lapsing of the Prime
Scintillates in oblivion's place!...
And yet the first word of his Verb:
ME!... Of stars the most superb
The mad creator ever said:
I am!... I will be!... I illuminate
The dwindling of divine estate
Of all the fires the Seducer spread!

Radiant target of my hate,
You whom I loved beyond perdition,
Who had to give the kingly state
Of Hell for such a love's admission,
Look at yourself within my dark!
Before your deathly image, mark
Of pride upon my sombre glass,
Where so profound your unease was
Your breath was, on the mirror's gloss,
A sigh of despair that was first-class!

In vain you have, out of the clay,
Shaped slapdash children made to give
You homage every day they live
For acts of Your triumphant sway!
No sooner shaped and given puff
Than Master Snake whistled 'em off,
The fine children You made so frail!
'Whoa!' said he, 'you greenhorns there!
You're men without a stitch to wear,
You beasts complacent and so pale!'

A la ressemblance exécrée,
Vous fûtes faits, et je vous hais!
Comme je hais le Nom qui crée
Tant de prodiges imparfaits!
Je suis Celui qui modifie,
Je retouche au cœur qui s'y fie,
D'un doigt sûr et mystérieux!...
Nous changerons ces molles œuvres,
Et ces évasives couleuvres
En des reptiles furieux!

Mon Innombrable Intelligence
Touche dans l'âme des humains
Un instrument de ma vengeance
Qui fut assemblé de tes mains!
Et ta Paternité voilée,
Quoique, dans sa chambre étoilée,
Elle n'accueille que l'encens,
Toutefois l'excès de mes charmes
Pourra de lointaines alarmes
Troubler ses desseins tout-puissants!

Je vais, je viens, je glisse, plonge,
Je disparais dans un cœur pur!
Fut-il jamais de sein si dur
Qu'on n'y puisse loger un songe?
Qui que tu sois, ne suis-je point
Cette complaisance qui point
Dans ton âme, lorsqu'elle s'aime?
Je suis au fond de sa faveur
Cette inimitable saveur
Que tu ne trouves qu'à toi-même!

Created in the image accurst
You were, and so my hatred is
For you as for the Name that first
Created impaired prodigies!
For I am He who modifies,
The heart that in its trust relies,
My hands retouch, mysterious, deft!...
These flabby deeds we will derange,
And these evasive vipers change
To savage reptiles, tongues cleft!

My Intellect, so Infinite,
Can finger in the human heart
An instrument for vengeance fit
And fashioned by your hands and art!
And your veiled Fatherhood, although,
Within its chamber's starry glow,
It culls but incense as it twines,
All the same, my excessive charms
Can vex with long, far-fetched alarms
All its omnipotent designs!

I come, I go, I plunge, I stream,
I vanish in the heart that's pure!
For was there ever heart so sure
That one could never plant a dream?
No matter who, aren't I the prick
Of satisfaction in the quick
Whenever soul loves self alone?
I'm at the source of all her favour;
I'm that inimitable savour,
Except within yourself, unknown!

Ève, jadis, je la surpris,
Parmi ses premières pensées,
La lèvre entr'ouverte aux esprits
Qui naissaient des roses bercées.
Cette parfaite m'apparut,
Son flanc vaste et d'or parcouru
Ne craignant le soleil ni l'homme;
Tout offerte aux regards de l'air,
L'âme encore stupide, et comme
Interdite au seuil de la chair.

O masse de béatitude,
Tu es si belle, juste prix
De la toute sollicitude
Des bons et des meilleurs esprits!
Pour qu'à tes lèvres ils soient pris
Il leur suffit que tu soupires!
Les plus purs s'y penchent les pires,
Les plus durs sont les plus meurtris…
Jusques à moi, tu m'attendris,
De qui relèvent les vampires!

Oui! De mon poste de feuillage
Reptile aux extases d'oiseau,
Cependant que mon babillage
Tissait de ruses le réseau,
Je te buvais, ô belle sourde!
Calme, claire, de charmes lourde,
Je dominais furtivement,
L'œil dans l'or ardent de ta laine,
Ta nuque énigmatique et pleine
Des secrets de ton mouvement!

Now that Eve, once, I surprised her
In her first thoughts, her lips apart
For the spirits as they were
Born from the swaying roses' heart.
To me that paragon appeared,
Her full flank with gold veneered,
Fearing neither sun nor man;
Offered up quite to airs so fresh,
The soul still dormant, under ban
To cross the sill into the flesh.

O massing of beatitude,
You are so lovely, worthy prize
You are, for every caring mood
Of all the good and all the wise.
It is enough, one of your sighs,
To draw them to your lips once more!
The most pure press there very poor;
The most enduring most bruised rise...
And me, you make me sympathise,
From whom again the vampires soar!

Yes! From my lookout in the grove,
Reptile with ecstasies of birds,
And while my chitter-chatter wove
Tissues of wiles and nets of words,
I drank you in, lovely and mute!
Clear, calm, your charm a lolling brute,
How furtively I mastered you,
Eye for the burnt gold of your wool,
The mystery of your nape, and full
Of secrets of your movement, too!

J'étais présent comme une odeur,
Comme l'arome d'une idée
Dont ne puisse être élucidée
L'insidieuse profondeur!
Et je t'inquiétais, candeur,
O chair mollement décidée,
Sans que je t'eusse intimidée,
A chanceler dans la splendeur!
Bientôt, je t'aurai, je parie,
Déjà ta nuance varie!

(La superbe simplicité
Demande d'immenses égards!
Sa transparence de regards,
Sottise, orgueil, félicité,
Gardent bien la belle cité!
Sachons lui créer des hasards,
Et par ce plus rare des arts,
Soit le cœur pur sollicité;
C'est là mon fort, c'est là mon fin,
A moi les moyens de ma fin!)

Or, d'une éblouissante bave,
Filons les systèmes légers
Où l'oisive et l'Ève suave
S'engage en de vagues dangers!
Que sous une charge de soie
Tremble la peau de cette proie
Accoutumée au seul azur!...
Mais de gaze point de subtile,
Ni de fil invisible et sûr,
Plus qu'une trame de mon style!

For I was present like a smell,
And like the redolence of thought
Of which one couldn't quite report
The treacherous depth and under-swell!
And me, you couldn't, callow, quell,
O flesh so softly, firmly wrought,
Without my driving you distraught,
To waver in the splendour's spell!
But soon I'll have you now, I bet.
You shift a shade now, silhouette!

(Superb simplicity must impel
In us immenseness of respect!
The candour that its eyes project,
Stupidity, joy, pride, guard well
The beauty of the citadel!
Let's see what hazards to confect,
And, by this art, the most select,
The pure-in-heart let us compel.
That is my force, that my finesse,
Means to my end, my own, oh yes!)

Now, with a blindly dazzling drool
Let's spin a tracery so light
Where, pupil idling, Eve, the cool,
Will snare herself with dangers slight!
How, laid beneath a silken load,
Trembles the quarry's skin that glowed
Acclimatised to blue alone!...
But with a gauze that lacks all guile,
Not with some certain thread unknown,
More than my trick of tongue or style!

Dore, langue! dore-lui les
Plus doux des dits que tu connaisses!
Allusions, fables, finesses,
Mille silences ciselés,
Use de tout ce qui lui nuise:
Rien qui ne flatte et ne l'induise
A se perdre dans mes desseins,
Docile à ces pentes qui rendent
Aux profondeurs des bleus bassins
Les ruisseaux qui des cieux descendent!

O quelle prose non pareille;
Que d'esprit n'ai-je pas jeté
Dans le dédale duveté
De cette merveilleuse oreille!
Là, pensais-je, rien de perdu;
Tout profite au cœur suspendu!
Sûr triomphe! si ma parole,
De l'âme obsédant le trésor,
Comme une abeille une corolle
Ne quitte plus l'oreille d'or!

«Rien, lui soufflais-je, n'est moins sûr
Que la parole divine, Ève!
Une science vive crève
L'énormité de ce fruit mûr!
N'écoute l'Être vieil et pur
Qui maudit la morsure brève!
Que si ta bouche fait un rêve,
Cette soif qui songe à la sève,
Ce délice à demi futur,
C'est l'éternité fondante, Ève!»

Gild, tongue, oh gild for her then the
Most dainty ditties that you possess!
Allusions, fables, with finesse,
And fine-honed pauses let there be,
Use everything to bring her harm:
Nothing that doesn't coax or charm
To lose herself within my schemes,
Docile upon those slopes that ply
To depths of azure pools, the streams
That make their downfall from on high!

Oh what a prose without a peer;
What spirit, wit, have I not tossed
In the dædalian softness glossed
Of that most marvellous ear!
Nothing of loss, there, was my thought;
All profit to the heart, keen, caught!
Triumph is certain if my sounds,
Haunting the treasure of a soul
As bee corolla, stay in bounds
Of that ear's perfect golden scroll!

'Nothing,' I whispered, 'is less sure
Than is the holy word now, Eve!
A living knowledge swells to cleave
Enormous fruit now grown mature!
Don't heed that Being old and pure
Who bans the taster you'd achieve!
If there's a dream your lips conceive,
This thirst that dreams of sap to thieve,
That pleasure, that prospective lure,
It's eternity melting, Eve!'

Elle buvait mes petits mots
Qui bâtissaient une œuvre étrange;
Son œil, parfois, perdait un ange
Pour revenir à mes rameaux.
Le plus rusé des animaux
Qui te raille d'être si dure,
O perfide et grosse de maux,
N'est qu'une voix dans la verdure.
– Mais sérieuse l'Ève était
Qui sous la branche l'écoutait!

« Ame, disais-je, doux séjour
De toute extase prohibée,
Sens-tu la sinueuse amour
Que j'ai du Père dérobée?
Je l'ai, cette essence du Ciel,
A des fins plus douces que miel
Délicatement ordonnée…
Prends de ce fruit… Dresse ton bras!
Pour cueillir ce que tu voudras
Ta belle main te fut donnée!»

Quel silence battu d'un cil!
Mais quel souffle sous le sein sombre
Que mordait l'Arbre de son ombre!
L'autre brillait, comme un pistil!
– *Siffle, siffle!* me chantait-il!
Et je sentais frémir le nombre,
Tout le long de mon fouet subtil,
De ces replis dont je m'encombre:
Ils roulaient depuis le béryl
De ma crête, jusqu'au péril!

She drank my every little word
And they were building a strange base;
Her eye would leave an angel's grace
To slip back to my boughs preferred.
The slickest beast that ever stirred
Who mocked you being so obtuse,
Perfidious, grossest evil, was heard
Only as voice the leaves let loose.
– But serious that there Eve, and how,
Who heard it underneath the bough!

'Soul,' I was saying, 'sweetest place
For all forbidden pleasures' play,
D'you feel or not love's sinuous grace
I from the Father stole away?
This Essence of the Sky, have I
Delicately ordained to try
For ends more sweet than honey... Do
Taste of the fruit... Now reach up higher!
To gather what you would desire
Your lovely hand was given you!'

What silence fluttered by a lash!
But what a sigh from the sombre breast
The tree with shade nibbled and pressed!
The other, a pistil, gave a flash!
'*Hiss, hiss!*' it sang to my panache!
And I could feel a shudder wrest
The whole length of my subtle lash,
The coils in which I was suppressed:
From crested beryl went the thrash,
Almost as far as being rash!

Génie! O longue impatience!
A la fin, les temps sont venus,
Qu'un pas vers la neuve Science
Va donc jaillir de ces pieds nus!
Le marbre aspire, l'or se cambre!
Ces blondes bases d'ombre et d'ambre
Tremblent au bord du mouvement!...
Elle chancelle, la grande urne!
D'où va fuir le consentement
De l'apparente taciturne.

Du plaisir que tu te proposes
Cède, cher corps, cède aux appâts!
Que ta soif de métamorphoses
Autour de l'Arbre du Trépas
Engendre une chaîne de poses!
Viens sans venir! forme des pas
Vaguement, comme lourds de roses...
Danse, cher corps... Ne pense pas!
Ici les délices sont causes
Suffisantes au cours des choses!...

O follement que je m'offrais
Cette infertile jouissance:
Voir le long pur d'un dos si frais
Frémir la désobéissance!...
Déjà délivrant son essence
De sagesse et d'illusions,
Tout l'Arbre de la Connaissance
Échevelé de visions,
Agitait son grand corps qui plonge
Au soleil, et suce le songe!

Genius! O long impatience! Face,
At last, that time has come to see
The naked feet flash out a pace
Towards new Knowledge from the Tree!
Marble aspires and gold cambers!
These blond soles in shades and ambers
Tremble on motion almost bent!...
She vacillates, that great urn!
From out of which will fly consent
From the apparent taciturn.

To pleasure you propose to take,
Dear body, yield, yield to the bait!
Let thirst for metamorphoses make
A chain of poses circulate
Round the Forbidden Tree and slake!
Come without coming! Don't walk straight,
But vaguely, weighed with roses, snake!
Dear body, dance... Don't meditate!
Sufficient cause is pleasure's ache
Here, for the course that all things take!...

Madness it was for me to take
Such barren joy: to watch the thresh
Of disobedience so quake
The pure line of a back so fresh!...
Surrendering instantly its essence
Of goodness and illusion there,
The Tree of Knowledge, its whole presence,
Tousled with visions its floating hair,
Shuddered its great bulk in a stream
Toward the sun and sucks in dream!

Arbre, grand Arbre, Ombre des Cieux,
Irrésistible Arbre des arbres,
Qui dans les faiblesses des marbres,
Poursuis des sucs délicieux,
Toi qui pousses tels labyrinthes
Par qui les ténèbres étreintes
S'iront perdre dans le saphir
De l'éternelle matinée,
Douce perte, arôme ou zéphir,
Ou colombe prédestinée,

O Chanteur, ô secret buveur
Des plus profondes pierreries,
Berceau du reptile rêveur
Qui jeta l'Ève en rêveries,
Grand Être agité de savoir,
Qui toujours, comme pour mieux voir,
Grandis à l'appel de ta cime,
Toi qui dans l'or très pur promeus
Tes bras durs, tes rameaux fumeux,
D'autre part, creusant vers l'abîme,

Tu peux repousser l'infini
Qui n'est fait que de ta croissance,
Et de la tombe jusqu'au nid
Te sentir toute Connaissance!
Mais ce vieil amateur d'échecs,
Dans l'or oisif des soleils secs,
Sur ton branchage vient se tordre;
Ses yeux font frémir ton trésor.
Il en cherra des fruits de mort,
De désespoir et de désordre!

Tree, great Tree, the Heaven's Shade,
Tree irresistible of all trees,
Seeking delicious fruits to seize
In feeble marbles, you who made
Such labyrinths by which confined
Glooms will lose themselves and wind
Into the sapphire of the light
Of everlasting dawn above,
Sweet escape, aroma, slight
Zephyr, or predestined dove,

O Singer, drinker secretly
From precious stones in deepest seams,
The dreaming reptile's cradle-tree –
Who gave Eve up to idle dreams,
Great Being, striving up to know,
Who, to see better, always grow
Towards the summons of your peak,
You who, in gold the purest, rouse
Your hardy arms, your heady boughs,
And, downwards, in the depths you seek,

You could repulse the infinite
That's made of nothing but your growth,
And from the tomb to nest of it
Could feel all Knowledge! But, in sloth
Of torrid suns' gold laziness,
This grand old amateur of chess
Comes to your boughs to writhe in torture;
His focus makes your treasure quiver.
He pressed in it death's fruit, giver
Of despair and of disorder!

Beau serpent, bercé dans le bleu,
Je siffle, avec délicatesse,
Offrant à la gloire de Dieu
Le triomphe de ma tristesse…
Il me suffit que dans les airs,
L'immense espoir de fruits amers
Affole les fils de la fange…
– Cette soif qui te fit géant,
Jusqu'à l'Être exalte l'étrange
Toute-Puissance du Néant!

With delicacy I hiss, I hiss,
Fine serpent, cradled in the blue,
And offer to God's glory, this:
The triumph of my sorrow due...
Enough for me if, in this air,
Vast hope from bitter fruit hung there
Frenzy the fellow sons of clay...
– That thirst which made you grow immense
Exalts as far as Being's sway
Oblivion's strange Omnipotence!

LES GRENADES

Dures grenades entr'ouvertes
Cédant à l'excès de vos grains,
Je crois voir des fronts souverains
Éclatés de leurs découvertes!

Si les soleils par vous subis,
O grenades entre-bâillées,
Vous ont fait d'orgueil travaillées
Craquer les cloisons de rubis,

Et que si l'or sec de l'écorce
A la demande d'une force
Crève en gemmes rouges de jus,

Cette lumineuse rupture
Fait rêver une âme que j'eus
De sa secrète architecture.

THE POMEGRANATES

Hard pomegranates, half split,
Yielding to excess in your fruit,
I see brows of peerless repute,
Bursting, with their discoveries lit!

If all the suns you underwent,
O pomegranates gaping wide,
Made you, crafted with such pride,
Cleave the rubies' integument,

And if the dry gold of the skin
Under demand of force within
Cracks into jewels red with juice,

The brilliant outburst of that rupture,
Makes a soul I once had muse
Again over its secret structure.

LE VIN PERDU

J'ai, quelque jour, dans l'Océan,
(Mais je ne sais plus sous quels cieux)
Jeté, comme offrande au néant,
Tout un peu de vin précieux...

Qui voulut ta perte, ô liqueur?
J'obéis peut-être au devin?
Peut-être au souci de mon cœur,
Songeant au sang, versant le vin?

Sa transparence accoutumée
Après une rose fumée
Reprit aussi pure la mer...

Perdu ce vin, ivres les ondes!...
J'ai vu bondir dans l'air amer
Les figures les plus profondes...

THE WINE LOST

One day I had into the Sea
(But on what shores no longer know)
As offering to vacuity,
Poured precious wine, a dash or so...

O wine, who wished you to be lost?
Perhaps I followed something divine,
Or some care of my heart it cost,
Dreaming of blood, spilling the wine?

Her customary transparency
After the rosy smoke, the sea
Regained, pure as elsewhere...

Wine lost, waves drunk!... I saw them bound
Into the bitterness of the air,
The figures that were most profound...

INTÉRIEUR

Une esclave aux longs yeux chargés de molles chaînes
Change l'eau de mes fleurs, plonge aux glaces prochaines,
Au lit mystérieux prodigue ses doigts purs;
Elle met une femme au milieu de ces murs
Qui, dans ma rêverie errant avec décence,
Passe entre mes regards sans briser leur absence,
Comme passe le verre au travers du soleil,
Et de la raison pure épargne l'appareil.

INTERIOR

A slave with almond eyes, burdened with gentle ties,
Changes my flowers' water, in the mirrors, flies
To lavish her pure touch on the mysterious bed;
Amid these walls a woman she has led
To wander through my musings unobtrusively,
And pass across my eyes, nor break their vacancy,
As the glass may pass across the sun without resort
Or need of reason's mechanism of pure thought.

LE CIMETIÈRE MARIN

Μή, φίλα ψυχά, βίον ἀθάνατον σπεῦδε,
ταν δ'ἔμπρακτον ἄντλεῖ μαχανάν.

PINDARE, *Pythiques* III.

Ce toit tranquille, où marchent des colombes,
Entre les pins palpite, entre les tombes;
Midi le juste y compose de feux
La mer, la mer, toujours recommencée!
O récompense après une pensée
Qu'un long regard sur le calme des dieux!

Quel pur travail de fins éclairs consume
Maint diamant d'imperceptible écume,
Et quelle paix semble se concevoir!
Quand sur l'abîme un soleil se repose,
Ouvrages purs d'une éternelle cause,
Le Temps scintille et le Songe est savoir.

Stable trésor, temple simple à Minerve,
Masse de calme, et visible réserve,
Eau sourcilleuse, Œil qui gardes en toi
Tant de sommeil sous un voile de flamme,
O mon silence!... Édifice dans l'âme,
Mais comble d'or aux mille tuiles, Toit!

Temple du Temps, qu'un seul soupir résume,
A ce point pur je monte et m'accoutume,
Tout entouré de mon regard marin;
Et comme aux dieux mon offrande suprême,
La scintillation sereine sème
Sur l'altitude un dédain souverain.

THE GRAVEYARD BY THE SEA

*Seek not, my soul, the life of the immortal ones; but
enjoy fully the resources that are within your reach.*

PINDAR: *Pythian Odes* III

This tranquil roof where the doves tread
Quakes among pines, among the dead;
There, Noon the just with fires composes
The sea, the sea, always restored!
O, after thought, what a reward
A look at the gods' calm discloses!

What pure deeds of fine glints consume
Many a gem of unseen spume,
And what peace seems conceived as so!
When on the deep a sun's at pause,
Pure works of an eternal cause,
Time sparkles, and the Dream's to know.

Sure treasure, simple shrine to Minerva,
Mass of calm and clear reserve,
Haughty Sea, Eye, under a woof
Of fire, concealing so much sleep,
My silence! ... In the soul a keep,
But thousand-tiled, ridged golden, Roof!

Summed in one sigh, Temple of Time,
To this pure point I make the climb,
And settle, ringed by seaward vision;
As to the gods my supreme gift,
The tranquil scintillation drift-
Sows on the height a sovereign derision.

Comme le fruit se fond en jouissance,
Comme en délice il change son absence
Dans une bouche où sa forme se meurt,
Je hume ici ma future fumée,
Et le ciel chante à l'âme consumée
Le changement des rives en rumeur.

Beau ciel, vrai ciel, regarde-moi qui change!
Après tant d'orgueil, après tant d'étrange
Oisiveté, mais pleine de pouvoir,
Je m'abandonne à ce brillant espace,
Sur les maisons des morts mon ombre passe
Qui m'apprivoise à son frêle mouvoir.

L'âme exposée aux torches du solstice,
Je te soutiens, admirable justice
De la lumière aux armes sans pitié!
Je te rends pure à ta place première:
Regarde-toi!... Mais rendre la lumière
Suppose d'ombre une morne moitié.

O pour moi seul, à moi seul, en moi-même,
Auprès d'un cœur, aux sources du poème,
Entre le vide et l'événement pur,
J'attends l'écho de ma grandeur interne,
Amère, sombre et sonore citerne,
Sonnant dans l'âme un creux toujours futur!

Sais-tu, fausse captive des feuillages,
Golfe mangeur de ces maigres grillages,
Sur mes yeux clos, secrets éblouissants,
Quel corps me traîne à sa fin paresseuse,
Quel front l'attire à cette terre osseuse?
Une étincelle y pense à mes absents.

As fruit melts in enjoyment's bite,
Changing its absence to delight
Within the mouth where its form dies,
I sniff here smoke my future brings;
To the soul consumed the sky sings
Change to the shores when tumults rise.

Beautiful sky, true sky, I change,
Look! After such pride, such strange
Lassitude, yet so full of strength,
I give myself to this shining space,
Crossing the dead in their dwelling-place,
My shade subdues me its frail length.

My soul exposed to solstice-fire,
I bear you, justice to admire
Of ruthless light! I give you, pure,
Back to your first place outright:
Look at yourself!... To give back light
Implies a half in shade obscure.

To me, in me, for me apart,
At the poem's source, next to the heart,
Between the void and pure event,
I wait my inner depth to resound,
Dark, bitter, sonorous cistern, sound
In the soul a pit yet imminent!

Feigned captive of the leaves, do you know,
Gulf gnawing this frail lattice-row,
Secrets dazzling my eyes shut blind,
What body drags me to its bound,
What brow draws it to this bone-ground?
A spark there brings my dead to mind.

Fermé, sacré, plein d'un feu sans matière,
Fragment terrestre offert à la lumière,
Ce lieu me plaît, dominé de flambeaux,
Composé d'or, de pierre et d'arbres sombres,
Où tant de marbre est tremblant sur tant d'ombres;
La mer fidèle y dort sur mes tombeaux!

Chienne splendide, écarte l'idolâtre!
Quand solitaire au sourire de pâtre,
Je pais longtemps, moutons mystérieux,
Le blanc troupeau de mes tranquilles tombes,
Éloignes-en les prudentes colombes,
Les songes vains, les anges curieux!

Ici venu, l'avenir est paresse.
L'insecte net gratte la sécheresse;
Tout est brûlé, défait, reçu dans l'air
A je ne sais quelle sévère essence...
La vie est vaste, étant ivre d'absence,
Et l'amertume est douce, et l'esprit clair.

Les morts cachés sont bien dans cette terre
Qui les réchauffe et sèche leur mystère.
Midi là-haut, Midi sans mouvement
En soi se pense et convient à soi-même...
Tête complète et parfait diadème,
Je suis en toi le secret changement.

Tu n'as que moi pour contenir tes craintes!
Mes repentirs, mes doutes, mes contraintes
Sont le défaut de ton grand diamant...
Mais dans leur nuit toute lourde de marbres,
Un peuple vague aux racines des arbres
A pris déjà ton parti lentement.

Full of a fire unfed, closed site,
Hallowed, earth fragment offered to light,
Composed of gold, of stone, tree-glooms,
This place I like, beneath flambeaux,
Where marble quakes on shades below;
The faithful sea sleeps on my tombs!

Fine bitch, rout the idolater! While,
In solitude, with shepherd's smile,
I graze a long time the white flock,
My tranquil tombs' mysterious sheep,
The prudent doves, quaint angels, keep
Away, and the vain dreams that mock!

Once here, the future's idleness.
Deft insects fret what's moistureless;
All's burnt, depleted, air-borne here,
Till who knows what strict essence last ...
Being drunk on absence, life is vast,
Bitterness sweet, and the mind clear.

Hid in this earth the dead are well;
It drains their mystery, warms their cell.
High Noon, Noon motionlessly blue,
That self-reflects and finds it meet ...
O perfect diadem, head complete,
I am the secret change in you.

Your fears you've just me to contain!
My doubts, remorse, constraints remain
The flaw within your lofty gem ...
But in their marble-laden dark,
A vacant race, in tree-roots stark,
Has slowly borne your part for them.

Ils ont fondu dans une absence épaisse,
L'argile rouge a bu la blanche espèce,
Le don de vivre a passé dans les fleurs!
Où sont des morts les phrases familières,
L'art personnel, les âmes singulières?
La larve file où se formaient des pleurs.

Les cris aigus des filles chatouillées,
Les yeux, les dents, les paupières mouillées,
Le sein charmant qui joue avec le feu,
Le sang qui brille aux lèvres qui se rendent,
Les derniers dons, les doigts qui les défendent,
Tout va sous terre et rentre dans le jeu!

Et vous, grande âme, espérez-vous un songe
Qui n'aura plus ces couleurs de mensonge
Qu'aux yeux de chair l'onde et l'or font ici?
Chanterez-vous quand serez vaporeuse?
Allez! Tout fuit! Ma présence est poreuse,
La sainte impatience meurt aussi!

Maigre immortalité noire et dorée,
Consolatrice affreusement laurée,
Qui de la mort fais un sein maternel,
Le beau mensonge et la pieuse ruse!
Qui ne connaît, et qui ne les refuse,
Ce crâne vide et ce rire éternel!

Pères profonds, têtes inhabitées,
Qui sous le poids de tant de pelletées,
Êtes la terre et confondez nos pas,
Le vrai rongeur, le ver irréfutable
N'est point pour vous qui dormez sous la table,
Il vit de vie, il ne me quitte pas!

To thick absence they've drained away,
The white absorbed by the red clay,
The gift of life has passed to flowers!
Where are the usual words of death,
The personal touch and each soul's breath?
Where tears once welled, the worm devours.

The shrilling yells of tickled girls,
Eyes, teeth, the moist lids, the curls,
The charming breast that toys with fire,
The blood that glows as lips expand,
The final gifts, the fending hand,
Rejoin the dance, to earth retire!

And you, great soul, do you hope for dream
Without these tints that lie and seem,
Which wave and gold make here for eyes
Of flesh? Will you sing as thin air?
Come on! All passes! I'm porous-ware,
Holy impatience also dies!

Mean immortality, black and gold,
Consoler fearfully laurelled, cold,
That makes of death a mother's breast,
Religious ruse and lovely lie!
Who does not know, who not deny,
That empty skull, eternal jest!

Tenantless heads, fathers deep-laid,
Weighed down with spadeful after spade,
Who now are earth nor know our tread,
The true rodent, worm none disproves,
Not yours that rest beneath slab roofs.
It lives on life; nor leaves my head!

Amour, peut-être, ou de moi-même haine?
Sa dent secrète est de moi si prochaine
Que tous les noms lui peuvent convenir!
Qu'importe! Il voit, il veut, il songe, il touche!
Ma chair lui plaît, et jusque sur ma couche,
A ce vivant je vis d'appartenir!

Zénon! Cruel Zénon! Zénon d'Élée!
M'as-tu percé de cette flèche ailée
Qui vibre, vole, et qui ne vole pas!
Le son m'enfante et la flèche me tue!
Ah! le soleil... Quelle ombre de tortue
Pour l'âme, Achille immobile à grands pas!

Non, non!... Debout! Dans l'ère successive!
Brisez, mon corps, cette forme pensive!
Buvez, mon sein, la naissance du vent!
Une fraîcheur, de la mer exhalée,
Me rend mon âme... O puissance salée!
Courons à l'onde en rejaillir vivant!

Oui! Grande mer de délires douée,
Peau de panthère et chlamyde trouée
De mille et mille idoles du soleil,
Hydre absolue, ivre de ta chair bleue,
Qui te remords l'étincelante queue
Dans un tumulte au silence pareil,

Le vent se lève!... il faut tenter de vivre!
L'air immense ouvre et referme mon livre,
La vague en poudre ose jaillir des rocs!
Envolez-vous, pages tout éblouies!
Rompez, vagues! Rompez d'eaux réjouies
Ce toit tranquille où picoraient des focs!

Love, perhaps, self-hate maybe?
Its hidden tooth's so close to me
That any names may serve instead!
It sees, it wants, it dreams, it touches!
It likes my flesh. Its living clutches
Possess my life even in bed!

Zeno! Cruel Zeno! In my marrow
Have you shot that wingèd arrow
That quivers, flies, yet flies no place!
Born by its sound, killed by its head!
Ah! the sun ... What tortoise-shadow shed
For soul, Achilles, still at full pace!

No, no! ... Stand up! Into the fresh
Era! This pensive form break, flesh!
The wind's birth, my heart, drink deep!
Sea-coolness breathed restores my soul ...
O salty strength! Let's run in the roll
Of waves and, from them living, leap!

Yes! Great sea of delirious gifts,
You, panther pelt, chlamys in rifts
With countless images of sun,
Absolute Hydra, drunk on your flesh
Of blue, who bite your bright tail's thresh
In tumult seeming a silent one,

The wind rises! ... I must try living!
The vast air flicks my book shut ... Driven,
The wave dares leaps of rock direct!
Fly off, bedazzled pages! Break,
Waves, break! With joyous waters quake
This tranquil roof where jib-sails pecked!

ODE SECRÈTE

Chute superbe, fin si douce,
Oubli des luttes, quel délice
Que d'étendre à même la mousse
Après la danse, le corps lisse!

Jamais une telle lueur
Que ces étincelles d'été
Sur un front semé de sueur
N'avait la victoire fêté!

Mais touché par le Crépuscule,
Ce grand corps qui fit tant de choses,
Qui dansait, qui rompit Hercule,
N'est plus qu'une masse de roses!

Dormez, sous les pas sidéraux,
Vainqueur lentement désuni,
Car l'Hydre inhérente au héros
S'est éployée à l'infini...

O quel Taureau, quel Chien, quelle Ourse,
Quels objets de victoire énorme,
Quand elle entre aux temps sans ressource
L'âme impose à l'espace informe!

Fin suprême, étincellement
Qui, par les Monstres et les Dieux,
Proclame universellement
Les grands actes qui sont aux Cieux!

SECRET ODE

Superb collapse, so sweet an ending,
Battle forgotten, what delight
As fine as in the foam extending,
Dance done, the polished body's might!

Never had such a glimmer yet,
As these summer scintillations,
Upon a brow beaded with sweat,
Fêted the victory celebrations!

But, touched by Dusk, this great physique,
Achiever of so many things,
That danced, broke Hercules, unique,
No more than massed rose-colourings!

Under the pacing stars, sleep sound,
Victor, in waning entity;
Inherent in the hero bound,
The Hydra spreads to infinity...

And what Bull, what Dog, what Bear,
What objects of huge victory's chase,
The soul, with no resources spare,
Imposes on to formless space!

Supreme end, scintillating light
That, universal to all eyes,
Through Monsters, Gods, proclaims the sight
Of the great feats that are in the Skies!

LE RAMEUR

à André Lebey.

Penché contre un grand fleuve, infiniment mes rames
M'arrachent à regret aux riants environs;
Ame aux pesantes mains, pleines des avirons,
Il faut que le ciel cède au glas des lentes lames.

Le cœur dur, l'œil distrait des beautés que je bats,
Laissant autour de moi mûrir des cercles d'onde,
Je veux à larges coups rompre l'illustre monde
De feuilles et de feu que je chante tout bas.

Arbres sur qui je passe, ample et naïve moire,
Eau de ramages peinte, et paix de l'accompli,
Déchire-les, ma barque, impose-leur un pli
Qui coure du grand calme abolir la mémoire.

Jamais, charmes du jour, jamais vos grâces n'ont
Tant souffert d'un rebelle essayant sa défense:
Mais, comme les soleils m'ont tiré de l'enfance,
Je remonte à la source où cesse même un nom.

En vain, toute la nymphe énorme et continue
Empêche de bras purs mes membres harassés;
Je romprai lentement mille liens glacés
Et les barbes d'argent de sa puissance nue.

Ce bruit secret des eaux, ce fleuve étrangement
Place mes jours dorés sous un bandeau de soie;
Rien plus aveuglément n'use l'antique joie
Qu'un bruit de fuite égale et de nul changement.

THE ROWER

to André Lebey

Pulling against the great river, endlessly my rowing
Tears me from laughing places, regretfully and loath;
Soul with your hands lumbered, holding oars in both,
The sky must yield to tolling of the slow waves flowing.

Heart hard, eye heedless of the beauties that I clout,
Letting around me flourish the rings of water swirled,
I want to break with wide sweeps the illustrious world
Of leaves and fiery light that quietly I sing about.

Trees over which I pass, broad silk simplicity,
Surface of painted boughs, perfection of the peace,
Tear through them, boat; impose on them a wash's crease
Which runs with greatest calm to raze the memory.

Never have your charms, day, never have your graces
Suffered so greatly from a rebel's self-defence:
Just as suns drew me out of childhood innocence,
I head towards the source where not a name leaves traces.

The whole and ample length of sinuous nymph in vain
Hinders my harassed limbs with her pure arms and hands;
I'll slowly break a thousand glassy ties and bands
And all the silver barbs of her naked power disdain.

This secret noise of waters, this river with its strange
Placing of my golden days in silken blindfold;
Nothing more blindly wears away the joy of old
Than does a noise of steady flight without a change.

Sous les ponts annelés, l'eau profonde me porte,
Voûtes pleines de vent, de murmure et de nuit,
Ils courent sur un front qu'ils écrasent d'ennui,
Mais dont l'os orgueilleux est plus dur que leur porte.

Leur nuit passe longtemps. L'âme baisse sous eux
Ses sensibles soleils et ses promptes paupières,
Quand, par le mouvement qui me revêt de pierres,
Je m'enfonce au mépris de tant d'azur oiseux.

Through annulated bridges, deep waters bear me far,
Vaults full of wind, of purling murmurs, and the dark,
They run over a brow they press with tedium's mark,
But whose proud bone is harder than their archways are.

Their night lasts a long time. The soul lowers her eyes
Under it, her sentient suns and her quick lids prone,
When, by the motion which redresses me with stone,
I thrust on, in contempt of such useless azure skies.

PALME

à Jeannie.

De sa grâce redoutable
Voilant à peine l'éclat,
Un ange met sur ma table
Le pain tendre, le lait plat;
Il me fait de la paupière
Le signe d'une prière
Qui parle à ma vision:
– Calme, calme, reste calme!
Connais le poids d'une palme
Portant sa profusion!

Pour autant qu'elle se plie
A l'abondance des biens,
Sa figure est accomplie,
Ses fruits lourds sont ses liens.
Admire comme elle vibre,
Et comme une lente fibre
Qui divise le moment,
Départage sans mystère
L'attirance de la terre
Et le poids du firmament!

Ce bel arbitre mobile
Entre l'ombre et le soleil,
Simule d'une sibylle
La sagesse et le sommeil.
Autour d'une même place
L'ample palme ne se lasse
Des appels ni des adieux...
Qu'elle est noble, qu'elle est tendre!

PALM

to Jeannie

An angel, with a fearful grace
Scarcely veiling the bright flash,
Set on the table at my place
Plain milk, new bread; and with a lash,
An eyelid, clearly sent to me
The sign of a prayer, a plea,
That says in speaking to my vision:
– Calm yourself now, be calm, keep calm!
Recognise the weight of a palm
Bearing its copious fruition!

For in as much as it may bend
To the abundance of its yield,
Its form will have achieved its end,
Its bonds by heavy fruit revealed.
Admire it quivering to respond,
And how the pliancy of a frond,
Which shares the hour, can separate
Without mystery, the drawing
Down to earth, the overawing
Of the firmament's great weight!

This lovely mobile arbiter
Between the shadows and the sun
Simulates a sibyl, as it were
The wisdom and the sleep of one.
Around a very similar place
The laden palm betrays no trace
Of tiring of requests, goodbyes...
How noble, how gentle she is!

Qu'elle est digne de s'attendre
A la seule main des dieux!

L'or léger qu'elle murmure
Sonne au simple doigt de l'air,
Et d'une soyeuse armure
Charge l'âme du désert.
Une voix impérissable
Qu'elle rend au vent de sable
Qui l'arrose de ses grains,
A soi-même sert d'oracle,
Et se flatte du miracle
Que se chantent les chagrins.

Cependant qu'elle s'ignore
Entre le sable et le ciel,
Chaque jour qui luit encore
Lui compose un peu de miel.
Sa douceur est mesurée
Par la divine durée
Qui ne compte pas les jours,
Mais bien qui les dissimule
Dans un suc où s'accumule
Tout l'arôme des amours.

Parfois si l'on désespère,
Si l'adorable rigueur
Malgré tes larmes n'opère
Que sous ombre de langueur,
N'accuse pas d'être avare
Une Sage qui prépare
Tant d'or et d'autorité:
Par la sève solennelle
Une espérance éternelle
Monte à la maturité!

How worthy are her services
Of recompense in the gods' eyes!

The light gold that she's murmuring
Sounds from a simple finger of air,
And with a silken armouring
Covers the spirit's desert lair.
An imperishable voice, the voice
She cedes to winds of sand whose noise
Waters her with its sprays of beads,
Serves also as her oracle,
And takes pride in the miracle
That sorrows sing out of such seeds.

Yet, though she's unaware of it
Between the desert sands and skies,
Each day that shines again supplies
Her with some honey, bit by bit.
Her sweetness reaches maturation
By bearing the divine duration
That does not count the passing days,
But rather hides them to produce
A concentration in the juice
Of all the fragrance of love's ways.

If sometimes then despair occur,
And if the rigour you adore
Will work, despite the tears you pour,
Only in shadows of languor's blur,
Do not accuse of miserly fare
A Sage that works hard to prepare
So much authority and gold:
For through the sap in the due time
An everlasting hope shall climb
And in maturity unfold!

Ces jours qui te semblent vides
Et perdus pour l'univers
Ont des racines avides
Qui travaillent les déserts.
La substance chevelue
Par les ténèbres élue
Ne peut s'arrêter jamais
Jusqu'aux entrailles du monde,
De poursuivre l'eau profonde
Que demandent les sommets.

Patience, patience,
Patience dans l'azur!
Chaque atome de silence
Est la chance d'un fruit mûr!
Viendra l'heureuse surprise:
Une colombe, la brise,
L'ébranlement le plus doux,
Une femme qui s'appuie,
Feront tomber cette pluie
Où l'on se jette à genoux!

Qu'un peuple à présent s'écroule,
Palme!... irrésistiblement!
Dans la poudre qu'il se roule
Sur les fruits du firmament!
Tu n'as pas perdu ces heures
Si légère tu demeures
Après ces beaux abandons;
Pareille à celui qui pense
Et dont l'âme se dépense
A s'accroître de ses dons!

Those days that seem to you like blanks
And wasted to the universe
Have keen roots in the desert's flanks,
To wind beneath them and disperse.
The comose substance that's preferred
By shadows can never be deterred,
Before the bowels of the earth
Are reached, from seeking in that dark
The deep waters that bid to arc
To summits towering from its girth.

Patience, have patience in this.
Wait patiently in the blue!
Every atom of silence is
Also the chance of ripe fruit, too!
The apt surprise is sure to spring:
A dove, a breeze will stir a wing,
And suddenly the sweet thrill seize,
A woman, leaning over, set
That rain falling without let,
In which you go down on your knees!

Look how a people now sinks down,
Palm!... unable not to! bent
Over the dust that scatters brown
Over the fruits of the firmament!
You have not wasted all these hours,
Though you feel lightened of your powers,
After such beautiful surrender;
Like those who give themselves to mind,
Whose spirit drains itself to find
An increase of its gifts to tender!

Other Pieces

LA FILEUSE

Lilia …, neque nent.

Assise, la fileuse au bleu de la croisée
Où le jardin mélodieux se dodeline;
Le rouet ancien qui ronfle l'a grisée.

Lasse, ayant bu l'azur, de filer la câline
Chevelure, à ses doigts si faibles evasive,
Elle songe, et sa tête petite s'incline.

Un arbuste et l'air pur font une source vive
Qui, suspendue au jour, délicieuse arrose
De ses pertes de fleurs le jardin de l'oisive.

Une tige, où le vent vagabond se repose,
Courbe le salut vain de sa grâce étoilée,
Dédiant magnifique, au vieux rouet, sa rose.

Mais la dormeuse file une laine isolée;
Mystérieusement l'ombre frêle se tresse
Au fil de ses doigts longs et qui dorment, filée.

Le songe se dévide avec une paresse
Angélique, et sans cesse, au doux fuseau crédule,
La chevelure ondule au gré de la caresse…

Derrière tant de fleurs, l'azur se dissimule,
Fileuse de feuillage et de lumière ceinte:
Tout le ciel vert se meurt. Le dernier arbre brûle.

THE SPINNER

Lilia ..., neque nent.

The spinner sits in the blue of the casement views
Where the melodious garden's dandling; speeding,
The old wheel whizzes till she's in a wooze.

On azure drunk, tired from spinning wheedling
Hair that evades her frail fingers, dreamy thing,
Her little head nods forward, hardly heeding.

A shrub and the pure air form a living spring,
Suspended in the light, its delicious pose
With fallen petals the idler's garden showering.

One stem, where the wandering wind comes to repose,
Bows a vain salute to its starry grace,
Dedicating the old wheel, resplendent its rose.

But the sleeper spins a lone yarn; a trace,
Mysteriously, of faint shadow self-twines,
Through her long sleeping fingers spun apace.

With an angelic indolence the dream winds,
And, ceaselessly, trusting the mild spindle, sways
The undulant hair to please the caress that binds ...

Beyond so many flowers, the azure foils the gaze,
Spinner that engirdling leaves and light enisle:
The whole green sky is dying; the last tree's ablaze.

Ta sœur, la grande rose où sourit une sainte,
Parfume ton front vague au vent de son haleine
Innocente, et tu crois languir... Tu es éteinte

Au bleu de la croisée où tu filais la laine.

Your sister, the great rose with saint-like smile,
Perfumes your vague brow with wafts of her full
Innocent breath. You sense you droop... You've faded while

In the blue of the casement you were spinning wool.

HÉLÈNE

Azur! c'est moi… Je viens des grottes de la mort
Entendre l'onde se rompre aux degrés sonores,
Et je revois les galères dans les aurores
Ressusciter de l'ombre au fil des rames d'or.

Mes solitaires mains appellent les monarques
Dont la barbe de sel amusait mes doigts purs;
Je pleurais. Ils chantaient leurs triomphes obscurs
Et les golfes enfuis des poupes de leurs barques,

J'entends les conques profondes et les clairons
Militaires rythmer le vol des avirons;
Le chant clair des rameurs enchaîne le tumulte,

Et les Dieux, à la proue héroïque exaltés
Dans leur sourire antique et que l'écume insulte
Tendent vers moi leurs bras indulgents et sculptés.

HELEN

Azure! it's me... From caves of death arrived
To hear the waves breaking with regular boom,
And see again the galleys in dawn spume
With a file of golden oars from dark revived.

My solitary hands summon the monarchs on
Whose beards of salt amused my spotless fingers;
I wept. They sang their obscure triumphs, singers
Of gulfs that dropped astern their boats, outgone.

The hollow conches, the clarions I hear
Martially time the flight of oars; the clear
Song of the oarsmen links in chains the din,

And the Gods high on the heroic prow,
In their ancient smile insulted by the spindrift
Stretch carved, indulgent arms towards me now.

AU BOIS DORMANT

La princesse, dans un palais de rose pure,
Sous les murmures, sous la mobile ombre dort;
Et de corail ébauche une parole obscure
Quand les oiseaux perdus mordent ses bagues d'or.

Elle n'écoute ni les gouttes, dans leurs chutes,
Tinter d'un siècle vide au lointain le trésor,
Ni, sur la forêt vague, un vent fondu de flûtes
Déchirer la rumeur d'une phrase de cor.

Laisse, longue, l'écho rendormir la diane,
O toujours plus égale à la molle liane
Qui se balance et bat tes yeux ensevelis.

Si proche de ta joue et si lente la rose
Ne va pas dissiper ce délice de plis
Secrètement sensible au rayon qui s'y pose.

IN SLEEP WOOD

The princess lies asleep in a palace of pure rose,
Beneath the milling shadows, in the murmurings;
And from the coral, dim near utterance grows
Whenever lost birds peck about her golden rings.

She never even hears the droplets as they slip,
Jingling the treasure of a century's voided days,
Nor on the vague forest the wind, flute-sounding, rip
Apart the susurration with the horns' shrill phrase.

Let long the echo leave the dawn a sleeper,
O, always ever nearer match with lissom creeper
That hovers over you, and strokes your shrouded eyes.

So closely to your cheek, so leisurely the rose
Will never squander such delights as these folds, plies
That sense the rays of sun in secrecy of repose.

LE BOIS AMICAL

Nous avons pensé des choses pures
Côte à côte, le long des chemins,
Nous nous sommes tenus par les mains
Sans dire... parmi les fleurs obscures;

Nous marchions commes des fiancés
Seuls, dans la nuit verte des prairies;
Nous partagions ce fruit de féeries
La lune amicale aux insensés

Et puis, nous sommes morts sur la mousse,
Très loin, tout seuls parmi l'ombre douce
De ce bois intime et murmurant;

Et là-haut, dans la lumière immense,
Nous nous sommes trouvés en pleurant
O mon cher compagnon de silence!

THE FRIENDLY WOOD

We thought pure things side by side,
Along the pathways where they led.
We held each other's hand and said
Nothing ... among dim flowers that hide;

We walked like an engaged pair
Alone, in the meadows' green night;
We shared that faery fruit, the bright
Moon, friend of mad ones, and there

And then we died upon the moss,
Afar, alone in the shade's soft floss
Of that wood's intimate murmuring air;

And up in the vast light, alliance:
Weeping, we found each other there
O my dear companion of silence!

LES VAINES DANSEUSES

Celles qui sont des fleurs de l'ombre sont venues,
Troupe divine et douce errante sous les nues
Qu'effleure ou crée un clin de lune… Les voici
Mélodieuses fuir dans le bois éclairci.
De mauves et d'iris et de mourantes roses
Sont les grâces de nuit sous leurs danses écloses
Qui dispensent au vent le parfum de leurs doigts.
Elles se font azur et profondeur du bois
Où de l'eau mince luit dans l'ombre, reposée
Comme un pâle trésor d'éternelle rosée
Dont un silence immense émane… Les voici
Mystérieuses fuir dans le bois éclairci.
Furtives comme un vol de gracieux mensonges.
Des calices fermés elles foulent les songes
Et leurs bras délicats aux actes endormis
Mêlent, comme en rêvant sous les myrtes amis,
Les caresses de l'une à l'autre… Mais certaine,
Qui se défait du rythme et qui fuit la fontaine,
Va, ravissant la soif du mystère accompli,
Boire des lys l'eau frêle où dort le pur oubli.

THE INCONSEQUENTIAL DANCERS

Those who are flowers of shade have come here, crowd
Divine and sweet, wandering under the cloud,
Brushed or formed by a moon-beam ... Here they flit,
Mellifluous, fleeting through the wood clear-lit,
Mallow and iris and the dying rose,
Are graces of the night their dances unclose,
That spread their fingers' fragrance on the air,
Become the blue, the depths of the woodland where
A tiny pool beneath the shadows gleams,
A pale treasure of eternal dew, it seems
From which vast silence rises ... Here they flit,
Mysterious, fleeting through the wood clear-lit.
As furtive as a flight of gracious lies
They tread the dreams of the flowers' closed eyes.
Their dainty arms, with movements in a drowse,
As if in dreams beneath the myrtle boughs,
Mingle caresses with each other ... One,
Breaking the rhythm, from the pool has run,
Thwarting the thirst for the perfected rite,
To drink the lily sip of oblivion's night.

from ALBUM OF EARLY VERSES

LES VAINES DANSEUSES

Celles qui sont des fleurs légères sont venues,
Figurines d'or et beautés toutes menues
Où s'irise une faible lune... Les voici
Mélodieuses fuir dans le bois éclairci.
De mauves et d'iris et de nocturnes roses
Sont les grâces de nuit sous leurs danses écloses.
Que de parfums voilés dispensent leurs doigts d'or!
Mais l'azur doux s'effeuille en ce bocage mort
Et de l'eau mince luit à peine, reposée
Comme un pâle trésor d'une antique rosée
D'où le silence en fleur monte... Encor les voici
Mélodieuses fuir dans le bois éclairci.
Aux calices aimés leurs mains sont gracieuses;
Un peu de lune dort sur leurs lèvres pieuses
Et leurs bras merveilleux aux gestes endormis
Aiment à dénouer sous les myrtes amis
Leurs liens fauves et leurs caresses... Mais certaines,
Moins captives du rythme et des harpes lointaines,
S'en vont d'un pas subtil au lac enseveli
Boire des lys l'eau frêle où dort le pur oubli.

THE INCONSEQUENTIAL DANCERS

The ones who are light flowers have come here,
Figurines of gold and svelte beauties, are near
Under a pale moon's iridescence... Here they flit,
Mellifluous, fleeting through the wood clear-lit.
Mallow and iris and the nocturnal rose,
Graces of night, under their dance unclose.
What veils of scent their golden fingers shed!
But the soft blue is leafless, the spinney dead,
And on the meagre pool it scarcely gleams,
A pallid treasure of ancient dew, it seems,
Where flowering silence rises... Yet here they flit,
Mellifluous, fleeting through the wood clear-lit.
Gracious to cherished flowers their finger-tips,
A moon-trace sleeps on their devoted lips.
Their marvellous arms, with movements in a drowse,
Lovingly loosen, under the myrtle boughs,
Their tawny tresses and embraces... Some,
Less rapt in rhythm, the harps' now distant strum,
Toward the shrouded lake step furtively on
To drink the lily sip of pure oblivion.

from SELECTED PIECES

LA FEUILLE BLANCHE

EN VERITÉ, UNE FEUILLE BLANCHE
NOUS DECLARE PAR LE VIDE
QU'IL N'EST RIEN DE SI BEAU
QUE CE QUI N'EXISTE PAS.
SUR LE MIROIR MAGIQUE DE SA BLANCHE ETENDUE,
L'ÂME VOIT DEVANT ELLE LE LIEU DES MIRACLES
QUE L'ON FERAIT NAITRE AVEC DES SIGNES ET DES LIGNES.
CETTE PRESENCE D'ABSENCE SUREXCITE
ET PARALYSE À LA FOIS L'ACTE SANS RETOUR DE LA PLUME.
IL Y A DANS TOUTE BEAUTÉ UNE INTERDICTION DE TOUCHER,
IL EN EMANE JE NE SAIS QUOI DE SACRE
QUI SUSPEND LE GESTE, ET FAIT L'HOMME
SUR LE POINT D'AGIR SE CRAINDRE SOI-MÊME.

THE BLANK SHEET

IN TRUTH, A BLANK SHEET
DECLARES BY THE VOID
THAT THERE IS NOTHING AS BEAUTIFUL
AS THAT WHICH DOES NOT EXIST.
ON THE MAGIC MIRROR OF ITS WHITE EXPANSE,
THE SOUL SEES BEFORE HER THE PLACE OF THE MIRACLES
THAT WOULD BE BROUGHT TO BIRTH IN LINES AND SIGNS.
THIS PRESENCE OF ABSENCE OVER-EXCITES
AND AT THE SAME TIME PARALYSES THE ACT BEFORE
RECOURSE TO THE PEN.
THERE IS IN ALL BEAUTY A FORBIDDANCE TO TOUCH,
THERE EMANATES FROM IT SOMETHING INDEFINABLY
OF THE SACRED
THAT ARRESTS THE MOVEMENT AND PUTS THE MAN
ON THE POINT OF ACTING IN FEAR OF HIMSELF.

NOTES ON THE POEMS

Dawn (p. 31)

This poem is in the same form as 'Palm', the last poem in *Charms*, a classical French stanza first used by Ronsard, though Valéry uses a shorter line to gain lightness and speed. Several adaptations of this form appear in his work. He said that these two pieces were originally one poem and that they flowed out of him with ease after he had stopped work on the alexandrine. It was still a matter of several weeks. Typically, he also reflected that he was cautious about poems that came with apparent ease.

Edgell Rickword, reviewing *Charmes* in the *Times Literary Supplement*, 1923, wrote: 'For pure lyricism it would be hard to equal the ode "Aurore".... It is a long poem, but as fresh as dew, and the verse flows with the same limpidity throughout.'

The Plane Tree (p. 37)

The stanza Valéry uses here is composed of two alexandrines alternating with lines of six syllables – that is, half the length of the alexandrine. The pentameter cannot be split evenly in an equivalent way so the alexandrine base has been retained.

p. 37, *l.* 5   The rhyme 'that' is a true rhyme with 'foot' if pronounced in its unaccented form.

p. 39, *l.* 4   The French word here translated 'branches' mean 'oars'.

p. 41, *l.* 15   The Horse in the penultimate stanza is a reference to the poetic Pegasus. An almost anticipatory image similar to that used for the beech here occurs in Edward Thomas's *Richard Jefferies*: 'muscular, smooth beeches, moulded like the flanks and limbs of immortal beauty'.

Canticle of the Columns (p. 43)

This amusing poem has many puns and jokes in the original. This version does not keep them quite in the same place but reflects the tone. It might be thought Valéry chose a short line to suggest a columnar form. The rhymes here imitate the playfulness in his. He sometimes waives the rule of the alternation of monosyllable rhymes with those ending in the muted final 'e'. This gives his poem a sense of terseness. The device can't be convincingly imitated in English so in order to suggest the terseness the syllable count is sometimes cut to five.

The Bee (p. 49)

p. 49, *l.* 4   The French word translated 'basket' has several senses: basket; wedding basket; flower-bed; a corbeil in fortifications.

Poetry (p. 51)

p. 51, *l.* 10   'white bonds' refers to hands and arms. The image occurs again in the opening line of 'Interior' (p. 131) but is translated somewhat differently. Presumably the hands and arms are bonds in tying us to the exterior world. In his 'Bad Thoughts and Others', Valéry said that the opposable thumb distinguished man from the apes. He then added: and the opposable soul.

p. 53, *l.* 7   The idea of the flight of the swan may allude to, or glance off, Mallarmé's 'Le vierge, le vivace, et le bel aujourd'hui' where the symbolic swan is trapped in the ice. *Cygne*, 'swan', is pronounced in French exactly the same as *signe*, 'sign'. There is no sensible English equivalent for this.

The Steps (p. 55)

Celebrated in France as one of Valéry's least cagey, most intimate pieces, it has also been interpreted as a poem about the arrival of inspiration, yet another of his poems about poems. The poet himself claimed it to be a poem purely of feeling.

The Sash (p. 57)

This celebrates sunset, a time of day Valéry seems always to have enjoyed. Dreamy and impressionistic, it is worth comparing with Baudelaire's 'Evening Harmony'. There is a passage on dance in Valéry's prose essay, 'Degas Dance Drawing', that gives some of Valéry's ideas on dance, particularly in the passage on the medusa. See also the note on 'The Inconsequential Dancers', p. 181.

The Sleeping Woman (p. 59)

One of Valéry's earliest poems here, a brilliant, intimate though distant sonnet with an 1890s feel.

Fragments of the 'Narcissus' (p. 61)

Valéry said of lines 48–55 ('What sweetness ... where evening shapes'; lines 23–30 on p. 63) that they were his most perfect success. He thought them void of ideas and the most achieved of his approaches to 'poésie pure', 'pure poetry'. (One may be tempted to reply these days that all words, whatever else they may be, are a species of 'ideas'.)

The Pythoness (p. 83)

Valéry claimed that this poem began as the *donné* which survives as line 5 of the text: 'Pâle, profondément mordue ...' He also remarked in an interview that his decision to use this approach to the classical stanza, mentioned in the note to 'Dawn', above, was based this time on the example of Hugo's treatment of the form.

Valéry was staying in a wooded area of l'Avranche overlooking a little wandering river that once a day had a tidal flow from the sea. The poem has something of that serpentine quality and the conclusion may be a glimpsing reference to the location.

The Sylph (p. 99)

This and the next poem have been interpreted as a contrasting pair, this on the wayward nature of inspiration and the next on the vagaries of intelligent development of it thereafter. The poem may also be taken as a gentle mockery of Valéry's exegetes. In form it is a short-lined sonnet.

The Insinuant (p. 101)

See first comment in entry above. Some commentators take this to be an outline sketch of the ideas developed in 'Sketch of a Serpent'.

The False Dead Woman (p. 103)

One of Valéry's few poems in free verse, this has not attracted many enthusiasts. It seems a rather artificial variation on the theme of 'The Sleeping Woman'. J. Soulairol wittily called the devices in the poem the games of a vehicle of genius. Valéry was, indeed, upset after the publication of *Charms* to find one critic claiming this poem the best in the book.

Sketch of a Serpent (p. 105)

This poem is full of rapid changes of register, the monologue of a serpent who thinks he has great 'street-cred'. Valéry quietly sends him up with some elaborate sound effects of sibilance and his favourite alliteration on 'v'. It is in the ten-line stanza that he liked to use: forms of it occur in 'Dawn', 'The Pythoness' and 'Palm'. Here he sometimes varies the rhyme scheme from verse to verse for variety and flexibility.

On page 116, first line, Valéry does rhyme on 'les', 'the'; so here (p. 117, first line) the rhyme is on the stressed form pronounced 'thee'.

The Pomegranates (p. 127)

The word 'soul' in the last verse must be taken to mean 'a state or stage of soul'. The same oddity is in the original.

The Graveyard by the Sea (p. 133)

Valéry speaks of this poem as starting with a wordless rhythm of ten syllables in his mind, with the division of four and six syllables.

The ten-syllable line was largely superseded for major works in French by the twelve-syllable alexandrine. To match Valéry's use of the earlier form this version has been done in iambic tetrameters as opposed to the usual pentameters. Unfortunately, particularly in this case, English verse cannot match the rather fixed caesuras of French. Valéry's are very skilfully organised; when a count of five syllables occurs in a line. it thus has an effect difficult to transfer to English by similar means.

This poem gave him more trouble than most. He declared it abandoned rather than finished and later considered that perhaps stanzas VI–VIII ('Beautiful sky, true sky ... a pit yet imminent!' on p. 135) should have been cut. Its origination seems to suggest the truth of one of Valéry's assertions: 'Beautiful works are daughters of their form which is born before them.' But he also remarked elsewhere that for him form *was* content. In his essay 'Concerning The Graveyard by the Sea', he also emphasized that there existed 'an ethic of form which led to endless labour'.

p. 133, *l.* 13   Minerva is the Roman name for Athena, goddess of wisdom. The final 'a' of the name here must be taken over metrically to complete the opening iambic of the following line – the next best thing that could be done to preserving the rhyme.

p. 135, *l.* 1   The opening grape imagery here seems an elaboration of Keats's grape in the last verse of his *Ode to Melancholy*.

p. 141, *ll.* 25–26   The first two lines of the final stanza are a nightmare for translators into English, offering small chance of sensible rhyme matches. Here is a syllable rhyme which was as close as could be found. Even then, 'Driven' is an addition developed from the context.

Allen Tate wrote of this stanza as a whole: 'If there is greater poetry in French or English in this century [the twentieth] than the last stanza I have not seen it.' Depending on how much he had seen, a mistaken impression, no doubt, but an indication of what a reputation Valéry once had in the English-speaking world.

The poet used a remark close to that in the opening line of the stanza, though distanced a bit by the third-person narrative, in an enclosure with a letter to Pierre Louÿs in 1890. Valéry wrote: 'The future seems rather screwed up to him. The necessity of having to work appals him, for he has always shuddered under regulation. *Cependant il faut vivre!*' Literally: *However, one must live!* Thirty years later he cut the 'however' and added *tenter*, 'attempt to' live – which has encouraged commentators to suggest for the remark in the poem various levels of profundity that seem as excessive as other scholars' suggestions for Shakespeare's 'Ripeness is all'.

Secret Ode (p. 143)

This was written by Valéry to mark the end of the First World War. The title has set exegetes off in all directions. The poem keeps its secret within the image of the warrior who appears to be either defeated or victorious or both.

The Rower (p. 145)

Retained in this version, the alexandrine, rhymed *abba*, is a very steady stately measure that may have been intended to match the steady determined rowing. The poem is one of Valéry's least favoured in France. It might be more cogent, less mannered, if the bridges involved were tunnels.

In the last verse, 'sentient suns' is a literary image for the eyes of the rower.

Palm (p. 149)

The original repeats the form of the opening poem, 'Dawn'. Exigencies of translation have led to a lengthening of line here. The poem at first seems to be Valéry developing his beloved image or symbol of the nature of a tree. In French, however, *palme* is a feminine noun so there may be some interplay of image with the speaker. Because of this the feminine pronoun has been used for the tree which may sound a bit odd in English. The poem is dedicated to Valéry's wife. The title 'Palm' may also touch on the idea of the victory palm: after the silence, after the wrestle with words and meanings, the book has been finished.

Monestier suggests the idea of the poem may have come to Valéry from the rhyming coincidence of *palme / calme* – fortunately virtually the same in English and French. Whatever the source for this idea, Valéry did remark that young poets are often driven to a rhyme by a thought while older poets often find a thought through a rhyme.

p. 151, *l.* 12   This idea is fairly close to Shelley's line in the 'Ode to a Skylark':

> Our sweetest songs are those that tell of saddest thought.

In *Julian and Maddalo*, he also wrote:

> 'Most wretched men
> Are cradled into poetry by wrong,
> They learn in suffering what they teach in song.'

The speaker, Maddalo, represents Byron.

p. 153, *l.* 22   'Palm' isolated at the beginning of line 2 of the last stanza would remind most French readers of Mallarmé's similar though more puzzling use to open line 6 of 'Don du Poème' ('Gift of the Poem'):

> Palmes! et quand elle a montré cette relique...
> ('Palms! and when she has shown this relic...')

OTHER PIECES

In Sleep Wood (p. 163)

A development of the theme of Sleeping Beauty and the myth of Daphne perhaps, this poem is an early parallel with 'The Sleeping Woman' (p. 59) in its quiet, sensuous contemplation.

The Inconsequential Dancers (p. 167)

Valéry was always fascinated by dance and wrote much about it, for example, in *Degas Dance Drawing* and in his Socratic dialogue, *Dance and the Soul*. In the course of this, ecstatic dance is seen as one of the few ways that the 'soul' can momentarily escape the sense of the quintessential tedium of mortal life as observed by the clear mind by permitting the body to be absorbed into a pure, totally inutile and induplicable act. The dialogue as a whole may indirectly cast light on some of Valéry's attitudes to dance and verse.

> *Phaedrus*: By all the Muses, no feet [those during the dance] have ever made my lips so envious of them.
> *Socrates*: So then, your lips envy the volubility of these astounding feet. You'd like to sense your words take their wings and vest your words with figures as lively as their leaps!'

– Though the next speaker tones this down with an ironic remark about pedestrian turtle doves. The dialogue also compares the dancer in full ecstatic movement to the mind/soul at full function and concludes that '... with the body as with the soul, for which the god, the wisdom, and the depths demanded of it, are, and only can be, moments, flashes, shreds of extraneous time, desperate bounds out of its own form.'

The Inconsequential Dancers (p. 169)

The source of this version of the previous poem was a selection Valéry himself made (*Morceaux choisis*, 1930). It is included here as a small indication of how he was always striving to change and improve his verse.

The Blank Sheet (p. 171)

This note is totally indebted to the researches of Jean-Pierre Attal whose essay, entitled 'La feuille blanche, Un Inédit(?) de Paul Valéry' ('The Blank Sheet, An Unpublished Piece(?) by Paul Valéry'), appeared in *Orpheus* 4 (Perros-Guirec, France) in 2004.

What appeared to be a previously uncollected piece by Valéry was referred to in Britain in an article by Francis Steegmuller who explained, in *The Times Literary Supplement*, 17 September 1976, how this overlooked and uncollected 'La feuille blanche' ('The Blank Sheet', 'The White Leaf') came into his possession as a typed sheet. It had been written in 1944 or 1945 and thus not long before the poet's death. Surprisingly, at this late stage of his life, Valéry still seemed to be concerned in a Mallarméan way with the pure blankness of paper and the perils of the creative process.

It is surprising to read this piece of free verse written so late in the poet's life. First because one expects some development in such an intellectual's view of the poetic process, not least, of his own. Further, one knows that free verse was a seldom chosen medium for Valéry. However, Jean-Pierre Attal points out in his article – to what must be some slight amusement to many an English reader – that the passage was written at the request of friends of Valéry who were in the business of making beautiful handmade papers, an interest of his. This gives an entirely different feel to the piece and suggests that it is centred prose in uppercase layout for the purposes of beautiful printing and presentation on expensive handmade papers. (Another interesting link with Wallace Stevens who would sometimes get his books bound in beautiful styles in France.)

Apparently, in 1944, Marcel Déléon, a delegate of the General Syndicate of Paper-Makers in France, had shown Valéry in the course of several conversations samples of their luxury handmade papers and suggested he might like to write something about them for the association's magazine, itself called *The Blank Sheet*. Valéry seems to have delivered the piece in 1945, the year of his death. But the magazine ceased publication at the end of the war and the text did not actually appear until 1948 in a special issue to celebrate the invention of the first paper-making machine. The full text was in fact a prose passage, a version of which follows:

The whiteness influences the touch-whiter-than whites, appeals to them, crazes them, and if their common maulers were tracing...

It drives in the same way some thousands of petty intellects, small wits whose turmoils, junketings, conflicts compose what they call SPIRIT.

The purity of the absolute irritates them and when they perceive *with our eyes* a sheet dazzling and unblemished they cannot keep themselves from wishing to fill with their combinations, their games and their celebrations this virgin shore offered for accomplishments, as they flatter themselves, in a world which endures.

They think to perform miracles on it but it is certain that they will sully it.

In truth, a blank sheet declares by the void that there is nothing as beautiful as that which does not exist. On the magic mirror of its white expanse, the soul sees before her the place of the miracles that would be brought to birth with lines and signs.

This presence of absence over-excites and at the same time paralyses the act before recourse to the pen.

There is in all beauty a forbiddance to touch, there emanates from it something indefinably of the sacred that arrests the movement and puts the man on the point of acting in fear of himself.

But at last the hand decides, and as a player risks a card on the table, a pawn on the chessboard, is brought to the purity given and to the integrity of the possible stroke – word or line – which will break the spell.

The luxury handmade papers contained delicate watermarked designs of flowers and so forth that would indeed be sullied or obscured by writing or drawing across them.

Index of French First Lines

Index of French Titles

Index of English First Lines

Index of English Titles

French Poetry translated by Peter Dale
IN BILINGUAL EDITIONS FROM ANVIL

Tristan Corbière: Wry-Blue Loves

'Corbière is hard-bitten, perhaps the most poignant poet since Villon, in very much Villon's manner', pronounced Ezra Pound. The chronically invalid son of a robust sea-captain and novelist father, Tristan Corbière (1845–75) published one book of verse and was virtually unheard of in his lifetime. He is an informal formalist, delighting in clashing registers of diction and outrageous puns. With pervasive self-mocking humour his poems combine a hopeless love, a grounded sea-fever, a ferocious ironic compassion and a savage sympathy with dogs and underdogs. As Peter Dale writes in his introduction: 'Above all, he is his own man, able to resist the blandishments of literary theory, social expectations, and the mollifications of religion.'

The book contains the entire *Les Amours jaunes* and a selection of Corbière's uncollected poems.

Poems of Jules Laforgue

'He is an exquisite poet, a deliverer of nations . . . a father of light', said Ezra Pound in 1918. Part symbolist and part impressionist, Laforgue was not only one of the most innovative and individual of French poets but also among the most entertaining. He died in Paris in 1887 aged just 27. Peter Dale captures the resourceful energy and panache of his poetry in translations which are by turns as playful, wild, clear, obscure and impossible as the French poems.

'[Dale] conveys much of the letter of the original as well as the spirit... The collection is hard to over-praise'
– D. J. ENRIGHT, *The Observer*

Poems of François Villon

François Villon was born in Paris in 1431. History records a life of destitution and ill health, robbery and murder, torture and exile. What became of Villon after his 32nd year is unknown, but the poems he wrote in just six years capture in witty, intelligent and candid verse the low and high life of Paris. Together they stand as a body of work with few rivals in the literature of his own or of any other country.

'The modernity of François Villon as well as the permanency of his genius have found in Peter Dale their best interpreter'

— LOUIS BONNEROT

'One despaired of ever finding anyone to "capture" [Villon] in English. But it's been done. Here it is. Hats off'

— LAWRENCE DURRELL